How to Be Happy Today and Everyday

With A New 7 Minutes Magical Plan

PRATAP C. SINGHAL, MD

How to Be Happy Today and Everyday
With A New 7 Minutes Magical Plan

Copyright PRATAP C. SINGHAL, MD © 2021

Happy Life Publishing, Belleville, NJ, USA

ISBN # 978-0-989 1417-5-8

LCCN# 2021902397

No part of this book may be reproduced in any form, by photocopying or by any other electronic or mechanical means, including information storage or retrieval systems, without the written permission from the author/publisher.

Disclaimer:

My main objective in writing this book is to inspire you to lead and enjoy the happiest and a better life, with the hope that it will also help to create a better and a happier world for the generation to come. I advise that you use your intelligence, knowledge and intuition alongside the information in this book, based upon your belief system and upbringing.

Although I have made every effort to make this book as accurate as possible, there still may be mistakes in the content or typography. Therefore, the author and the publisher shall assume no liability or responsibility to any person or entity with respect to any loss or damages caused or alleged to have been caused directly or indirectly by the information contained in this book. Hence, the purchaser/reader must assume full responsibility for the use of the book or the information therein.

Dedication

This book is dedicated to the creation of a happier world. Let us begin with you and me and then let others join later, one at a time.

Mission: Smile a lot, laugh a lot, be happy, and let us try our best to put smiles on others' faces.

Pratap C. Singhal

About the Author

PRATAP C. SINGHAL MD, is a happiness coach and passionate about happiness. He is also known by the nickname 'Happy man'. He believes that the success of life can be best measured by one of these important criteria i.e., 'how happy a person is', because happiness encompasses most important elements of life and is a sign of maturity and wisdom.

Dr. Singhal is a physician who practices conventional and complementary medicine. The field of complementary medicine includes Homeopathy, Medical Hypnosis, Maharishi Ayurveda and Nutrition. He is also a specialist in helping people quit smoking.

He has shared this multifaceted expertise as a guest on several radio and television shows, and is also the author of other books titled, *Health, Happiness and You: Everything You Need to Know*, previously titled *Live Healthier, Live Happier (With the Help of 101-plus Suggestions, Formulas, Poems, Mantras, and the Lessons Learned from Short Stories)*, and *One Solution To Many Diseases, Presented in 24 ½ Inspirational Stories*. In 2017 he was interviewed on television; the interview can be seen on YouTube or at his website. In 2018 he was awarded the Hypnosis Research Award by the National Guild of Hypnotists, the largest Hypnosis organization in the world.

Dr. Singhal stresses the point that every human being should appreciate how precious his/her life is and should take full responsibility for its growth, development, and rise as well as physical and mental well-being, and therefore should work towards achieving that goal. This creates the foundation for everlasting happiness.

Appearance on the magazine cover.

He was pictured on the magazine cover- titled '**Journal of Longevity**'

1st time in December 2014-- volume 4/No 29/Gardavita.com

2nd time same Journal in 2014 vol. 07/no. 50/Gardavita.com

He was also interviewed by local TV for 28 minutes, and you can watch the whole interview at his website www.pcsinghalmd.com

Acknowledgements

I wish to thank wholeheartedly those who have inspired and encouraged me to write this book, especially those who have given positive feedback on my previous books.

I also wish to take this opportunity to thank those people who are responsible for the shape, and position I am in today. Firstly, my mom and dad, the great souls, for their wisdom, love, care, for instilling into me the values of human life, especially giving me plenty of exposure to the greatest spiritual master of the time.

To my wife Sushum, for encouraging me to study homeopathy and natural medicine, and for sharing the work and responsibility at home and work so that I can spend time on my book.

I must acknowledge my three sons Arun, Sunil, and Dhruv, and their spouses, and eight grandchildren (at the time of writing this book). Since my last book, we have two new arrivals, Bodhan, and Avi. The whole family including all grand-children namely Kieran, Meera, Sonia, Sarin, Sarina and Kalyan welcomes them with open arms.

To my brothers and sisters and their spouses for being part of my life: one could not ask for any better.

To all my friends and relatives: I have honored them in my first book and I honor them again here.

I would like to thank my patients, friends, and family members who have shared their inspirational stories with me with an open heart and allowed me to publish them, without which this book could not have been possible.

I am proud to be on the medical staff of Clara Maass Medical Center in Belleville, New Jersey, a great facility dedicated to the care of the sick and injured. It is named after a nurse named, 'Clara' named who gave her life for the benefit of humanity.

I also thank Ms. Ritu Chopra, author, writer, speaker, and TV hostess for her support. I also thank Dr. Richard Nongard for his expert publishing advice.

My special thanks to my two dear nephews, Vikram Singhal and Vivek Singhal, for their invaluable support and making suggestions and reviewing the manuscript.

I would like to apologize to those whose names I might have missed inadvertently.

Pratap C. Singhal

Table of Contents

Introduction and, A New 7 Minutes Magical Plan. What is the new 7 minutes magical plan?... 1

Section One : Fifty- Seven Amazing Secrets from the Happy and the Wise 8

Section Two : The Twelve Amazing Secrets from the Unhappy, Naïve and Miserable Ones 153

Section Three : The Fourteen amazing Tenets of the "Law of Nothingness" 184

Section Four : The Last Amazing Secret: Choose and Act 209

Appendix : The Art of Happiness 212

The Happiness Poem 225

Until Next Time — Namaste 232

Bibliography 233

Books by the Author 234

Introduction and, A New 7 Minutes Magical Plan. What is the new 7 minutes magical plan?

If you ask me, is this book for me? I will say yes, of course. Since you have opened the book it means you are in search of happiness. I can assure you that there is no better place and time than now. So, take this opportunity and you will be happy that you did. If I have to say in a nutshell, I would say this book is your ticket for the plane ride to the happy land.

This book has several unique features. I shall name the top three for now.

Firstly, this book is unique in the sense that it is not based upon any hypothesis, or philosophy. It is rather based upon practical life examples of people like you and me who have faced many tough challenges of life and met them successfully without losing their happiness. They have set up the example and shown the path step-by-step, that you could all tread and follow.

The 2nd unique feature about this book is that I have formulated the 'Law of Nothingness'. A very short path to happiness. It is so brief you could read the whole section in half an hour and it will uplift your happiness level. I have collected this information from our Scriptures. I have discussed this in the 3rd section of the book.

The 3rd unique feature is reflected in the subtitle: New 7 minutes magical plan.

What is the new 7 minutes magical plan? This plan involves programming your magical mind for the happiest life ever.

You all know the fact that the mind runs your life. It makes all the decisions on your behalf. You do whatever your mind tells you to do. Your mind is the most powerful and wonderful element that you have. It is equally important to understand that your mind is your friend.

But there is something more important than that, that is in as much as your mind has control over you, you also can control your mind. In other words, you can tell your mind what to do. However, it requires some programming on your part. This is how you do it:

For 7 minutes a day, every day you will be choosing happiness. You will be making a commitment for happiness. You know the important life principle i.e. 'You choose what you want and you will get what you choose.' Just think what you are today, most likely you will agree that this is what you had chosen to be sometime in the past. That is a basic principle of life. To reiterate, you get what you choose.

Next, coming to the practical side of programming, it requires 7 minutes a day. I have divided these 7 minutes segments into 3 parts of 2+2+3 minutes each.

The 1st segment of 2 minutes should be devoted to recalling and remembering the good happy days of the past and of childhood. Here, you will smile, laugh, make faces and have fun. I strongly recommend that you use a mirror to see your smiling and happy face during those 2 minutes.

The 2nd segment of 2 minutes, is devoted to self-reflection. You know that the self-reflection is the key for growth, betterment and making positive changes in life. What to reflect upon?

You will be reflecting and thinking of new ideas as to how to make life happier each and every day. On day one, it may be a little difficult to come up with a new idea, but this process becomes easier and easier everyday thereafter. The reason being as you will be reading this book every story will give you new ideas/new insight.

The 3rd and the last segment of 3 minutes is devoted to the reciting of the mantras that I have created for you. The mantra should be recited 6 times a day and each time spending no more than half a minute.

Following is the mantra that you need to recite:

"I am a happy person and happiness is my second nature. When I think of my childhood, I remember vividly how happy, carefree, and full of life I was. This brings pleasant memories and gives me the feeling of nostalgia, and I feel overjoyed and energized. Therefore, from this moment on, I shall work to bring that happiness back into my life and I shall protect it in my heart and soul. I know I can do it."

Let me reiterate once again, that this should not take more than a half a minute each time.

What are the best times to recite the mantra?

The 1st two times are, the first time when you open your eyes in the morning, the last time just before you go to bed.

Next 2 times are, just before any two important meals of the day. It could before breakfast and dinner or it could be before lunch and dinner.

The remaining 2 times are, when you leave home for work or doing any other chore and the 2nd time when you return home. Good enough!

I hope you have been following so far; therefore, I believe that your mind is magically ready and prepared to accept and choose happiness.

Before going a little further, I should make some comment about the powerful and interesting title of the book, 'How to be happy today and Everyday'. What a beautiful goal to aim for life. Can you imagine what your life would be if you're happy every day of your life? You will be full of energy, excited and maybe floating around at least mentally. You will be an example of happiness. People will love you. It is also equally important to understand that learning happiness is an easy and pleasant process. The only element required is having a mindset for which you are already set.

Next, coming to the content of the book. Please note that the reading of the book is also rewarding and fun because these are interesting/or challenging life stories of real people. Some stories are so interesting you may forget to eat or sleep. I strongly recommend that you read the book the first time in 30 days for maximum benefit. However, you may like to read it again in future for deeper and better insight.

I also want to re-emphasize here that happiness is a choice. You will appreciate that from the following. You know there are two classes of people, one who are always happy and upbeat and the other always miserable. You need to know that the lives of these two classes of people may not be much different, they may be living in the same house in the same circumstances, but it is the choices that these people have made in the past that make all the difference.

Sometimes I wonder why there are so many unhappy people? The fact is that the road to happiness is a little difficult and tedious, and it requires patience and understanding however, it is a rewarding path. Whereas, the road to unhappiness is a shortcut and an easy path. That is the reason why so many people fall into this trap.

If you were to ask me, Why another book on happiness? My friends, happiness is such an important subject that there can never be enough literature on the subject, because who knows who can benefit from which one. Just imagine if this book could uplift your level of happiness even just a little, then you will thank yourself for investing in this book. Further as mentioned earlier, this book has so many unique features that you cannot find anywhere.

To stress upon you the importance of happiness, let me give you two examples. For comparison's sake, recall two days of life: one day when you were very happy, and another when you were sad and/or miserable. Next, compare the feeling that you get by just thinking of those different days. You see the difference, how the happy day gives you more energy and joy, just thinking about it. Such is the importance of happiness. Also, when you're happy your day goes fast and smoothly, and when you are sad it is a drag.

Let's take another example; think of the feeling you get when you meet a few happy people versus a day when you meet some sad people. Again, compare the feelings. I'm sure you can appreciate the fact that on the day when you meet happy people, you are more energized, and of course the reverse is also true.

Let me say a few words about the layout of the book. This book has been divided into the four sections.

In the very first section you will learn from the lives of happy people. I have met these people in my personal and/or professional life as a physician over several decades. You will appreciate how these people have worked very hard to keep and protect their happiness; and how they have used human values to their advantage such as positive attitude, acceptance, forgiveness, love, hope, faith in the self, faith in God, and so on. Each story will amaze you — at times your mouth will remain open for a while when you read these stories — and more importantly, you will benefit from it.

In the second section, you will learn from the unhappy and the miserable ones. You will appreciate how these people have become victims of circumstances by giving into negative elements such as greed, anger, jealousy, hatred, anxieties, worries and so on. It is an example of ignorance or lack of insight. You will learn a lot from those stories as well. I shall explain to you how, little later.

In the third section I have dealt with the law of nothingness. What is the Law of Nothingness? It is the essence of my understanding of how to achieve a happier life. A path. A guide in brevity.

In the fourth and the last section, there is a special message for you. This is the shortest section, but an important one.

I have also included a bonus chapter at the end of the book titled, The Art of Eternal Happiness. I have taken this chapter from my first book, Health Happiness and You—Everything You Need to Know. I believe that you will enjoy and benefit from that.

You know well that happiness is a vast subject. The more you travel on this path, the more you would like to travel. This book is just an addition to that vast subject of happiness. I sincerely believe that the information in this book will uplift you and your happiness level to a degree that will impact your life in a positive manner. I also believe that the more intently you read this book, the more you will benefit from it. I also believe you can increase your happiness level more by sharing the information with others, because in this way not only you are helping others but it also provides an opportunity to remind yourself what you have read in this book till the information in this book becomes your second nature. It is a known fact that when you help others, you also feel happier inside because you have done something good to someone. You must agree that it also uplifts your heart and soul.

Finally, I suggest you put on your seatbelt, take 3 deep breaths, have a great smile, think of something best that happened to you and be ready for the plane ride to the happy land.

I wish you all the best in your pursuit of a journey to a happier life that you have been waiting for a long time. Please go for it.

Thank you very much.

Pratap C. Singhal

Section One

Fifty- Seven Amazing Secrets from the Happy and the Wise

This section contains 57 amazing secrets/stories. Since each story is unique and will leave a permanent and positive impression on your mind, I would therefore like to label them as model stories. Remember that each secret is based upon the real-life stories of average people like you and me. These people have chosen happiness, despite the difficulties and challenges of daily life, from which no one is exempt. You cannot fail to miss how hard they have worked to preserve their happiness.

Secret #1. Want to be happy? Who is stopping you?

Secret #2. What a father says to God at the death of his very young son. This will keep you thinking for a long time?

Secret #3. The positive attitude and its unbelievable power!

Secret #4. The appreciation: one of the biggest boosters of happiness!

Secret #5. Just change yourself and the world will change in a flash.

Secret #6. Should you be happy?

Secret #7. Catch them, and don't let go.

Secret #8. What was the life of a slave like?

Secret #9. How does one slave become very rich? — an intriguing story

Secret #10. This one powerful word could put an end to any argument?

Secret #11. Why does evil grow faster than the mushrooms?

Secret #12. Happiness is balance, and unhappiness is misery — how and why?

Secret #13. Are you listening to your friendly Guardian Angels?

Secret # 14. How partial information can hurt you?

Secret #15. Conscience and happiness: the important link!

Secret # 16. Intentions versus outcome: who wins?

Secret #17. Why is everybody just a number in this vast universe?

Secret #18. How deep faith in God and the self helps people to go through tough times?

Secret #19. Awakening!

Secret #20. The present is too precious to waste on the past issues of life!

Secret #21. The "Joy and Blues" of holidays.

Secret #22. When loss or win, has no meaning?

Secret #23. How a wise old man meets death's challenge?

Secret #24. When death knocks at the door: how a patient responds?

Secret #25. Which is the single most precious gift of all?

Secret #26. You are not the problem!

Secret #27. My experience of working at the psychiatric hospital for one week.

Secret #28. When 'happiness' also has to go in search of happy people?

Secret #29. Adaptability and flexibility — two amazing secrets of happiness.

Secret #30. Tolerance and acceptance — a tribute!

Secret #31. Acceptance/ Gratitude.

Secret #32. Contentment!

Secret #33. What comes around goes around — a bona fide truth?

Secret #34. Should you ever retire? A big question

Secret #35. A too-busy life: a curse or a blessing?

Secret #36. How big is your heart? How can yoy measure it?

Secret #37. Stress — the necessary evil!

Secret #38. How to take advantage of a catalyst?

Secret #39. How to benefit from 'Anchoring'

Next are some secrets from the wise:

Secret #40. 'Needs' and 'Wants', the ongoing war between them and how it affects you?

Secret #41. Why did Mahatma Buddha [The Prince] abandon the luxury of the palace to become a monk?

Secret #42. How to stop others from bothering you?

Secret #43. The actions are wise, and the reactions foolish!

Secret #44. How a wise man wins, the hate with love? — a true story

Secret #45. How high is the life of a person — the measuring unit?

Secret #46. Simple living and high thinking: a spiritual model

Secret #47. A brief interview with a Lama on the subject of life

Secret #48. Is there a fastest way to learn happiness?

Secret #49. The power of the commitment to a healthy and happy life!

Next are some spiritual secrets:

Secret #50. Meditation: a path to happiness.

Secret #51. Silence: the time for inner reflection and self-growth.

Secret #52. Prayer: one of the best ways to charge one's life batteries.

Secret #53. The curse of a golden pen.

Secret #54. The power of the mighty truth!

Secret #55. Should you forgive?

Secret #56. Put smiles on their faces and they will put one on yours.

Secret #57. Yoga: the science of life's mastery, and laughing yoga.

Secret #1: Want to be happy? Who is stopping you?

"Folks are usually as happy as they make up their mind to be."
— *Abraham Lincoln.*

This is a powerful and true statement coming from one of our greatest presidents.

Here is another quote from a great swami and Yogi, Swami Paramahansa Yogananda:

"If you want to be sad, no one in the world can make you happy. But if you make up your mind to be happy, no one and nothing on the earth can take that happiness from you."

Yes, if you want to be happy nobody has the power to stop you, nor will stop you from being happy. It is your own game. Everything in this universe is set up for the happiness and well-being of all. Right from the beginning of the arrival of the man on this earth till the present time. When man 1st arrived, Scriptures were created and their teaching is focused for the happiness and well-being of all. And today the Constitution of the country has the same philosophy. As a matter of fact, everybody wants you to be happy that includes your parents, family friends and well-wishers and so on. Let me say this message in the poetic language:

In this vast world of abundance,

there is plenty of everything:

happiness to misery,

joy to sadness,

the good to the best

and the bad to the worst.

So,

Choose what you want,

and you will get what you choose.

(Here is one piece of good news — if somebody does not wish to be happy, or wishes to remain sad, it is okay, in the sense that it is not against the law and nobody can prosecute or arrest you for that.)

This is also my observation: that happy people are happy, just because they have made up their mind to remain happy. It does not matter whether this decision is made at the conscious or even subconscious level. Further, it has been observed that happy people exist at all levels of life. For example, some are rich, others poor; some are educated, others illiterate; some male and others female, some from a higher social status and others from the lowest social status, and so on. In other words, money, education, sex, social status etc. are not prerequisite for happiness.

Allow me to share an anecdote about one of my patients:

Ms. KP has been my patient for more than 30 years. Her family has had to deal with multiple challenges in life, although they are financially okay. Whenever I ask my patient how she is, she will typically reply with a smile and in a pleasant tone, "People are as happy as they make up their mind to be. So, I'm okay."

Here is another example: one of my friends was a very happy man and used to say, "I am determined to remain happy, and there is no way in the world that anyone can take my happiness away. You really must kill me to take my happiness away, because I am determined to remain happy under all situations, circumstances, and all times."

Finally, to impress upon you the importance of mindset, programming and choosing happiness especially at an early upbringing, I will show you something interesting that you will benefit from. Recently, I was visiting one of my closest family members, I noticed the following mission statement that hung in their well-lit kitchen. I took the consent of the family to print it here. Here is the mission statement:

The mission statement of the family

We are a family that laughs so hard we cannot stop

We are a family that loves, hugs and sticks together

We learn from each other

We do hard things

We do the next right thing

We take care of our bodies by eating healthy and being active

We are explorers

We are a welcoming family

We give back

This mission statement is so powerful that I must have glanced at it several times during my weekend visit to the family. Can you imagine how often the family must have looked at it? What positive effect it would have on the mind or even the lives of the children? Can you make this mission statement as part of your life?

Next, I like to answer two extremely important questions before coming to the end of the chapter because these questions have been raised by many people from time to time. They are as follows:

The first question that people have asked me is, 'Am I entitled to happiness?' Many people have the impression that because they did not go to school or colleges, or do not believe in God, or they do not have a high social status, they may not be entitled for happiness. However, according to our Scriptures every human being is entitled for happiness. Therefore, I have devised a test to clarify that point.

The Test: Are you entitled for happiness?

I have devised this test for your insight. It has only six questions. (You do not have to agree with the results.) It is just a simple and fun test, with nothing to it.

1. Are you born on this planet? Y/N
2. Are you between the age of one and one hundred-plus? Y/N
3. Are you male, female or have any sexual orientation? Y/N
4. Have you ever had a good laugh lasting for more than one minute? If not, are you willing to do so now, even if you have to tickle yourself? Y/N
5. Do you want happiness in your life? Y/N
6. Are you willing to sacrifice some small issues to preserve your happiness? Y/N

If you have answered all the questions affirmatively, then you do qualify for happiness. However, if you did not, do not be discouraged.

In this world of happiness, everybody gets a second chance. Pause and take the test again when you are ready.

The second question that people have asked me is -'What happiness really means'? I think it is important to discuss this subject because happiness means different things to different people. Therefore, I like to clarify that point.

What happiness really means?

There are several definitions of happiness as given by the Oxford English Dictionary. I think the best one is "the feeling or showing of pleasure and contentment."

In the next few lines, I have tried to clarify what happiness means and/or does not mean.

1. Happiness does not mean that the problems of life will go away because they may not, but it means that you will be able to solve them gracefully.

2. Happiness does not mean that you will not have ups and downs in life because you may, but it means you will maintain your balance during those times.

3. Happiness does not mean that there is nothing that can bring you down, but it means that you will bounce back faster than before.

4. Happiness does not mean that someone may not attempt to knock you down because someone may, but it does mean that you will be able to stay firm and strong on your feet.

5. Happiness does not mean that people will not criticize you because they may, but it means you will not be affected by the behaviors of others like before.

6. Happiness does not mean that you will have no pain (physical and mental) because you may, but it means you will not suffer, at least not for long.

7. Happiness does not mean just laughing, giggling or feeling slap-happy but it means calm, content, collected and balanced.

8. Happiness does not mean that you must wait for eternity, but it means it is here and right now.

Most important of all, happiness means that you will be holding the key to it in your own hand, firmly and strongly for as long as you wish. Here is a poem that I have created to reinforce the above message:

The Poem: World of Abundance — You Choose What You Want

This is the world of abundance

Here you will find plenty of everything.

Happiness to misery

and joy to sadness,

good to the best and

bad to the worst.

My friend, please remember,

Hell, and heaven are also here.

So, choose what you want and

You will get what you choose.

There are people of all kinds.

This world is rich with generosity and kindness.

Cruelty and meanness are also here big time.

Cheating, meanness and the stealing of dimes.

So, choose what you want and

You will get what you choose

One day in the month of June

I was on a beach.

It was a beautiful day full of sunshine.

Neither was it too hot, nor too cold.

The beach was filled with people;

Children, ladies and men of all kinds.

You could hear the giggling and laughing of the children.

Balloons in one hand and chocolate in the other

they were licking ice cream and running around here and there.

Their faces were filled with joy and innocence.

They were lost in their own little world.

As I looked a little way down the beach,

children were playing, making sand houses and

collecting pebbles,

keeping their parents busy and reminding them of their own past.

For a moment I thought,

If this is not heaven,

then it is nowhere.

But when I turned my attention to the other side of the beach,

I saw an angry madman.

He was mad like hell.

He must be the father of the little boy

Who was crying, begging and following this mad man?

This man was also collecting red pebbles one at a time.

He would pick up a pebble and if it was red, he would put into his bag,

however, if it was not red, he would toss it angrily back into the sea.

Why he was mad,

what made him mad,

nobody will ever know;

I dared not ask.

Because he was mad like hell.

Then I thought, *this is hell.*

My friend, please remember,

hell, and heaven are all here.

Says Pratap, see with your eyes or with your mind,

it is all here; it is all here.

Let me say finally, make the following two lines the song of your life.

Choose what you want and

you will get what you choose.

Let me add little extra to that:

If you can breathe, laugh, and laugh a lot.

If you have a face, smile, and smile a lot.

And If you have a soul, be happy at all times because it is the seat of happiness.

After reading the above you should be able to appreciate the power of the mind set for happiness!

If you need further proof, read the next story with your open heart. After that you will not need any further convincing.

Secret #2. What a father says to God, at the death of his very young son? This will keep you thinking for a long time.

Have you ever been to the funeral of anyone, or a condolence meeting, especially if it involves the loss of a young life? Typically, people come home with a heavy heart, sadness and/or drag. However, this story is unique, in the sense that it provides you an insight and a positive way of looking at such a difficult scenario. Here is the story:

Dr. D is a dear friend of mine and was my classmate in medical school. We each got married and we each have three children. As time went on, we got even closer to each other because his children and mine were of similar ages, and they used to play with each other. Later, my friend moved to another state because of the job situation, and we were not in touch with each other for a while.

So, life continued and one of his sons became a doctor, too. On the day of his graduation from medical school, his father gave him a great party with all the pomp and show. After the party was over, everybody went outside to go home. A taxi was called.

As the taxi came to pick his son and the family, it could not stop. The taxi crushed and killed his son on the spot, on the very first day of being a doctor. (Who knew that he was born to be a doctor, just for one day?)

I did not know this incident until much later. Thereafter, I went to see my friend to offer my condolences. I said to him, while looking deep into his eyes, "My dear friend, I am shocked to hear about your son's death. This is not fair. I know how you must feel."

My friend kept looking intently into my eyes, took a long pause before he replied. Then he said:

'We cannot be angry at God, and we cannot blame him. I am still thankful to God that He gave us our son for 26 years."

After hearing this statement, I became quiet. I was amazed and could not believe what my friend had said. I kept looking at him a little more deeply and intently, and he also kept looking at me. I think he was waiting to see how I would respond to his statement. Eventually, I nodded my head in agreement. I could not say any more.

However, I could not get over his statement for a long time. I kept wondering how much thought he must have given and how much pain he must have swallowed before making such a profound statement. His words left a deep impression on my heart and I could not admire him enough.

On that night, I slept at his home. I kept thinking of the statement that he has made that

'We cannot be angry at God, and we cannot blame him. I am still thankful to God that He gave us our son for 26 years."

That night, I told my wife what my friend had said firstly, she could not believe it and then she said, your friend is a great human being.

It so happened that the next day I had to give a presentation on 'Happiness' in a large gathering, and I brought up the story of my friend and the conversation that I had with him. Finally, I quoted his exact statement:

'We cannot be angry at God, and we cannot blame him. I am still thankful to God that He gave us our son for 26 years."

His statement was one of the few elements of my talk that created feeling of 'Awe' in the audience.

Thereafter, one of the attendees from the audience stood up and said,

Dr. Singhal, your friend is right, 'We take everything for granted. We often blame God, and forget to thank him what so many other things He has given us.

Secret #3. The positive attitude — it's unbelievable power!

Christian minister Charles Swindoll has stated: "I am convinced that life is 10% what happened to me, and 90% how I react to it. And so, it is with you. You are in charge of your attitude."

[It is only partial a quote]

You may have experienced the power of positive attitude in your life, and how it can affect the lives of others. You may have observed yourself on many occasions that although people may be living under similar conditions or circumstances, while some are happy, thankful and feel fortunate, others are unhappy, miserable and even feel unfortunate. It is all due to one thing: attitude.

Let me share an interesting story of three laborers to explain this fact. The story goes like this:

There was a temple under construction and three laborers were working outside side-by-side. It was the hot month of July in India.

A spiritual master was passing by and he asked one of the laborers, "What are you doing?"

The first laborer replied in resentment and anger, "Sir, I thought you were an educated person. Can't you read the sign that states that the temple is under construction? Therefore, please go, and don't waste my time. I must get to work."

The spiritual master walked about 10 feet and asked the second laborer the same question: "What are you doing?"

The second laborer replied, "Sir, I am an uneducated person and I cannot read or write anything. I do whatever they tell me to do. I have given a job to cut the stones and that is what I'm doing. I do not know anything more than that. I must feed my family and this job is helping me to do that."

Next, the spiritual master walked another 15 feet and asked the third laborer the same question: "What are you doing?"

The third laborer stood up to honor the master, then spoke respectfully and said, "Sir, a temple is being built here. I feel very fortunate and blessed to be a part of this holy project. Every time I think that people will come here to pray, and I am contributing something to that, I feel overjoyed. This gives me a lot of energy. For the grace of God, I feel lucky that I got this job.

When you analyze this story, you can appreciate that all the three laborers are doing the same job and getting paid the same wages. However, the last laborer, who has a positive attitude, is feeling blessed, but the very first laborer, who has a negative attitude, is miserable, and the second laborer, whose focus is just to make a living, is surviving and nothing more.

Such is the power of attitude. I call the positive attitude an ornament of life, that beautifies life and brings a lot of joy and happiness.

My friends, think have you ever observed the power of the positive attitude in your life?

Secret #4. The appreciation: one of the biggest boosters of happiness!

Appreciation and Appreciation!

You know most people face quite similar difficulties and challenges in life. However, some people enjoy life and others curse it. I shall show you by several examples the one secret that can make all the difference.

Last week while making hospital rounds, I commented to a nurse that I always saw her happy and the patients liked her very much. I asked her, what is her secret?

She replied, "Dr. Singhal, I do not know what to tell you, except that I am married for 40 years and have two children and we are a close-knit family. We all care about each other. Financially we are doing okay. We have no big issues in life. We appreciate everything that we have. God has been good to us. That is all, and nothing more. I just happen to be one of the luckiest people."

This also must have been one of those special days for me, because I had just finished talking to the nurse and was still thinking about what she had said. I got up to continue my hospital rounds, and when I entered the room of my first patient, she welcomed me with a smile. I asked her why she was so happy; this patient had been in a wheelchair for more than 10 years.

She replied, "I am happy because I am a very lucky person. I know I cannot walk, but I have eight children and 20 grandchildren and each one of them gives me a lot of love and energy that makes my life worthwhile. I can't ask for anything more."

On my last visit to India in 2017, I was socializing with my nephew, and he said, "Uncle, when you are having a good life and you do not appreciate it in thoughts or words, you are not sincere to yourself and to the Almighty, who has provided us all those things."

Here is another story of one of my patients. Mr. WM has been my patient for 20 years and is now 75 years old. He always has a happy demeanor. I asked, "Mr. WM, tell me — what is the secret of your happiness?"

He replied, "Dr. Singhal, I am so grateful to God for all that he has given to me. I'm healthy and still alive, whereas most of my friends are dead. Therefore, I must be doing something right. Every morning when I open my eyes the very first thing that I do is touch and feel myself, and I get amazed every day that I'm still able to see, hear, feel, touch and walk on this earth. Of course, I'm also happy by nature. What else do you need at this age!"

Recently I bought a new car and I was very impressed with the spirit of the salesperson. He was joking and laughing all through the sales process. I commented to him that he seemed to be very happy. He replied, "Yes, if I'm above the ground, I'm happy. Who knows after death?"

'Appreciation' is the key word. Appreciation can bring one so much closer to happiness than one cannot imagine or believe. Those people who do not appreciate life enough do not know what they are missing.

Secret #5. Just change yourself and the world will change in a flash!

'The outer world is a reflection of your inner- self'

One question, three perspectives. Here is a small but an interesting incident that will reinforce the above statement.

For me, it was a typical day going to the hospital. After parking my car in the doctors' lot, I started to walk to the hospital when I met three friends, all fellow doctors, in a matter of minutes, one after another. Strangely enough, all three doctors asked me the same question but then made comments based upon their own perception of me.

Somehow on that day I was walking with my head down, I do not remember why, but that is not important here. I had not walked even 20 yards from my car when I met Dr. C and he asked me, "Dr. Singhal, are you okay? Cheer up; things are not as bad as you think." I just smiled in response.

After going another 50 yards, I met a second colleague of mine, Dr. F, and he asked me the same question. "Dr. Singhal, are you okay? Did you forget something?"

I had walked another 90 yards when I met a third doctor friend, Dr. P, and he also asked me, "Dr. Singhal, are you okay, or are you just lost in deep thought. Are you working on your next book?"

For your information, Dr. C. had a history of depression, therefore his comment was advising me to cheer up, things are not as bad as you think. Dr. F has a problem with forgetting things, and often has to go back to the car to get some equipment, so he asked me did you forget something. And the third friend, Dr. P, was a philosopher type. He did his best thinking when walking. Therefore, his question was, are you lost in your thoughts. Each of my friends made comments based upon their own inner perception.

So, although the world is the same, different people perceive it differently, based upon their own personal understanding of the world. Therefore, people ask questions and interpret the answers from their own perspective.

Happy people perceive that everybody is happy and life is wonderful, whereas sad people perceive that the whole world is sad and it is falling apart. The fact remains that, "the outer world is the reflection of the inner self."

Secret #6. Should you be happy?

Normally, you would think that everybody wants to be happy in life or strives for happiness. However, I have learned that is not always the case.

One day I asked one of my patients, "Are you happy?" (This is a routine question that most doctors would ask a patient during a physical.)

She replied, "Are you supposed to be happy? I thought you're supposed to eat, live and work, and maybe have a family and that is it."

I was kind of stunned by the answer. I could not comprehend why she said that or what her background might be. Then I came to the realization that happiness is not a word in the dictionary of many lives. That is a little sad. Thereafter I told her yes, we are supposed to be happy in life. We do everything in life for our happiness. This is the teaching of the not only our ancestors but also of our Scriptures.

Next let me tell a story in contrast to what she said. Once I was visiting a swami (spiritual master) at his ashram in India. For my family, this was a yearly routine to get some spiritual knowledge during our vacation time. (An ashram is a place where a swami lives and imparts spiritual knowledge to the people who visit them. It is their contribution to society, and there is no fee for that.)

During that visit, Swami gave a great sermon. It was half an hour long, but the core message was "Enjoy life and be happy, otherwise, God may not be happy with you. Because when you're happy, you are following his command, and when you're not happy, you're acting against his wishes."

He clarified the message further; he said that God is our heavenly father. We feel happy when we see our children happy, and we also feel unhappy or even sad when we see our children sad. In those situations, we question ourselves as parents: why is my child not happy when I am doing my best to give the child whatever he or she needs?

The swami continued, it is the same or similar with God. He has the same relationship with us as we have with our children. He does not like to see us unhappy. He wants us to enjoy life and be happy, that is why God has provided us with everything, including the knowledge that we need in life to survive, in the form of Scriptures. (My understanding is that our scriptures are the manuals for life.)

You should be happy not only because God wants you to, but also because when you're happy and enjoying life you can overcome many hurdles and miseries more easily and life can become easy sailing. In addition to that, you may rub happiness off on others — that will make this world a better and a happier place to live in for everyone. Of course, that will include you.

Secret #7. Catch them, do not let go.

This is a very interesting and educational piece of information however, let us have a little fun for a change, before going to the real topic.

I want to show you the power of the comma in English, or in any language. Based on the title above, you will understand the meaning of the phrase- catch them, not let go. It implies catch them. However, if you change the location of the comma, the meaning reverses totally. This is the fun part. Let me rewrite the above phrase by changing the location of the comma. Here it is:

Catch them not, let go.

You noticed that now have inserted the comma after "not", when before it was after "them". You can appreciate that now the meaning has been reversed. Now it means, don't catch them. The message is exactly the opposite of what was initially intended, just because of the location of the comma. The only interesting lesson which this anecdote gives you is, that one must be very careful where to put commas in a sentence.

Let's go back to our real topic. Catch them, not let go.

You know there are a lot of good people in this world. However, people who are good and happy are hard to meet in one's life. When you find such a person or persons, catch them, and do not let go. Stick with them, shadow them, make friends with them or serve them if you have to. Learn from them; it will make a big difference in your life. Make them your role models. That will bring joy in your life.

Personally speaking, I have a learned a lot from such people and it has colored my life tremendously. I can say that I am fortunate enough to be part of such a family. My parents and all my siblings had given precedence to happiness in all aspects of life.

Not only this, when I went to high school, I had a couple of good friends who were also very happy. This was pure luck. And when I went to college, again I met few good and happy classmates who made all the difference in my life. So much so that every day I became more and more interested in furthering research into the subject of happiness. As a matter of fact, this is one of the reasons that I wrote this book. Following this practice can also do great things for you.

Secret #8. What was the life of a slave like?

"I was a slave one day" — Mr. Z

Did you ever think about what the life of a slave was like? How did they live? The following story provides an insight into such a life.

Mr. Z had been my patient for more than ten years. He was 96 years old. During one of our office visits, being impressed with his demeanor, and his degree of tolerance and acceptance, I happened to ask him, "Mr. Z, what work did you do in your life? How did you make your living?"

Mr. Z replied, "Dr. Singhal, I was a slave."

I was shocked by his statement and I became quiet. I felt a little awkward and guilty about why I had asked this question. It took me a few moments to absorb what he had said. I kept looking at him for a quiet moment, and he kept looking at me. I was staring at him with a kind of guilt about asking the question, and he was waiting to see how I would respond to his answer.

To break the silence, I summoned a little courage and asked him, "What was the life being a slave?"

He replied, "Dr. Singhal, we ate and worked, that was the life. There were no choices, there was no place for questioning. I have come to understand that what you cannot change, you must accept. I was thankful to God for whatever I got."

I had noticed that he was never demanding and was appreciative of everything. Even if somebody would offer him a cup of tea, he would thank the person several times. I like to cite an example of his behavior to give you just a little clue of his level of tolerance. I had observed that he always came to my office without an appointment, although I had told him several times that he should not do that. (He had to catch two buses from his home, to get to my office.)

It so happened that on two different occasions he decided to visit me at the office, but my office was closed. When he came for his next appointment, he told me what had happened. I said I was sorry. He said no, you do not need to feel sorry, I should have called before coming, as you have been advising me. Therefore, it is my fault, and I cannot blame you for that. He was not angry or annoyed for not making the appointment. I also noticed that this incident did not change his behavior and he continued to come to the office without an appointment.

One day I asked, "Mr. Z, why don't you make an appointment before coming?"

He replied, "Dr. Singhal, you are a busy man and I don't want to waste your time with unimportant phone calls. And moreover, I have nothing important to do. I am just a retired person." This is how he was. That was him!

Let me give you an important quote:

Change what you can, accept what you can't, and be smart enough to know the difference. —Wally Lamb.

However, I must stress the second part of the statement, that if something can be changed, it should.

I will also share an interesting phrase from my school days. During those years, my friends used to console each other with the following phrase:

For every problem in this world, either there's a solution or none. If there is one — go find it, and if there is none — never mind it.

The author is unknown. This is equivalent to the statement that we still often say, "What cannot be cured must be endured."

Secret #9. How does one slave become very rich? — an intriguing story

Here is another insight into the life of a slave! It is quite different from the first one.

This is the story of a 60-year-old lady who came to me as a patient. I got to know her well only after two or three visits. She had a happy demeanor. I asked her the same routine question that I ask many of my happy patients: tell me the secret of your happiness?

She replied, "Dr. Singhal, I'm a happy person by nature. Although I was a slave for 40 years from the age of 20 till my owner died. But there are two elements that I want you to know about my life. Firstly, my owner had no children. Secondly, not only he was wealthy but was a kind and loving person.

"In his life, he treated all his slaves very well, like his own children. Not only this, he wrote in his will that all his estate should be divided equally among his slaves, and I got a pretty good share of it. I have no qualms about life. As a matter of fact, I took my last name after him."

After reading this story, you must come to realize that happiness exists in the hearts of many, especially those who know how to make the best of life. One's education, wealth, social status, age, sex, or even the events of the past are not the criteria for or barrier to happiness.

The second message is that nature's ways are mysterious. How one can go up so high or even so low in life in no time?

A word about slavery: Slavery is a crime and it is a universal truth. And everybody knows that. However, slavery has not stopped yet. It continues at the worst level even today. Human trafficking is such an example. If slavery would stop, this world would be a heavenly place and the people would be like God. Just give that some thought.

Secret #10. This one powerful word could put an end to any argument!

Once I was at a social gathering and with about twenty other people. There was a discussion about religion. As you know, the subject of religion can be very controversial. Mr. RS was one of the better educated people in the group and he expressed his views openly. However, there were five people who did not like his views. They kind of got angry with him. They told him emphatically that he was wrong and started to argue with him.

He calmed down the whole situation just with one statement. This is what he said:

"I am not here to convince or change any one of you. This is my opinion and you have a right to have your own."

The effect of this statement was like putting water on fire. Nobody said a word after that.

One needs to remember that a discussion on any controversial subject such as religion, politics, or anything of a similar nature can become a cause for argument. Of course, the best thing is to avoid such a discussion. However, if you do get caught in this situation, you know how to get out of it.

Let me say something which is related to this. Some people try to change others' opinions, or even try to convert others to their faith or religion. This can become a source of discord or even start a fight. You need to know that change is not easy for anyone; that includes you. So, if you cannot change yourself, then how can you expect others to change?

I have come to understand that confrontation or arguments are like a little battle between two people, where nobody wants to lose, and yet nobody wins.

Secret #11. Why does evil grow faster than the mushrooms?

Resolve all issues or problems early on, before they get too big.
— My father

This was one of the philosophies that my father preached and practiced, not only at home but also at work. He was a businessman and, on many occasions, he had to settle several deals with little gain or even a slight loss. His philosophy was, just move on and don't get stuck on any one issue. However, he did stress the point that one should never compromise principles and ethics while making a settlement. I also observed that on many occasions when it became a question of principle or ethics, he did not mind going an extra mile to prove his point.

He also used to say that "by going to the court you may win the case at times, but in the long run when you look back the money, energy and time invested, and many restless days and sleepless nights that went with it, more often than not you will come to realize that it was no-win, and at times you may even repent over it."

At home, he followed the same philosophy. He used to say that if you have a disagreement or even a little misunderstanding with a family member, you must resolve the issue before you go to bed. In this way, not only you will have a good night's sleep, but also the other dear family member will appreciate and respect you for your act. The other member will give you a higher place in his or her heart. My father's point was that the longer an issue lingers, the bigger the shape it can take.

You know, evil is evil. It grows faster than the mushroom because it has too many legs. It definitely grows faster than goodness. You also know that at times evil can be so powerful that it may take several good elements to kill one bad one, depending how bad it is. Therefore, nipping the evil in the bud and putting an end to its growth is a great philosophy.

Secret #12. Happiness is balance, unhappiness is misery. How and why?

Neither be too sweet like sugar, nor be too bitter like a poison.
— My mother

This was my mother's favorite phrase that she used often. It has a deep underlying meaning. One day I asked my mother to explain to me what she meant, and she replied: "When you are too sweet with someone, you may get so much attached to the person that you may forget or even compromise your own principles and ethics, and someday that might get you into trouble. Equally true is the fact that when you are too bitter with anybody, you will make enemies, and nobody wants to make enemies. Just remember the extremes of both can be bad for you."

Although above is a small statement but it has a deep message embedded in it. The message is balance. You all know the importance of balance. Balance in life is extremely important for mental well-being and happiness. Whereas imbalance can be a cause of misery, suffering and unhappiness. Remember that the balance and imbalance can be at any level; that includes physical, mental, emotional, and spiritual and so on.

To clarify the matter further, you need to know that most element has three levels of existence. The normal, high, or even low. For example, blood pressure of a person can be normal, or it can be high or low. A person can be of normal weight or he/she can be of underweight or overweight. To give you another example healthy people have a normal blood glucose that is the example of balance. However, when the blood glucose is either low or high it is abnormal. When blood glucose is low it is called hypoglycemia and when it is high it is known and diabetes mellitus.

The following is an additional list of balances and imbalances from the practical life that will make the matter clearer and interesting. Also remember that there are some funny examples in this list that will make you laugh. I have borrowed this list from one of my previous writings. I believe you will enjoy and benefit from it.

Physical level

1. Some people have overly dry skin; others have overly oily skin. Some people cannot perspire at all; they go to a sauna and exercise to perspire just a little. Others perspire so much that they need to change their clothes two or three times a day.

2. Some people have such a dry nose that they must carry saline mist at all times; others have a constantly runny nose and are never without a tissue.

3. Some people have very little hair or are bald, while others have hair all over their body, including on the face, nose, and forehead, making them look like a bear.

4. Some people cannot digest even the simplest of foods while others eat like a horse—as if the food is going to run out.

5. Some people chew so slowly that you'd think they do not like the food or are already full. Others eat quickly, as if somebody will snatch their food (as most carnivorous animals do).

6. Some people are always sleepy or are not satisfied even after ten to twelve hours of sleep. Others can't sleep even ten to twelve hours in a week because they are so restless, hyper, and nervous.

7. Some people have no desire for sex; their partners wonder if something is wrong with them and why they can't attract their partners. Others want so much sex that they drive their partners crazy.

8. Blood pressure is either too high (hypertension) or too low (hypotension); both conditions need treatment.

9. Blood sugar is either too high (diabetes) or too low (hypoglycemia); both conditions need treatment.

10. Thyroid glands are either overactive (hyperthyroidism) or underactive (hypothyroidism); both require treatment.

11. Some people walk so fast that the person in their company thinks that he/she is being ignored. Meanwhile, others walk as slowly as if they are exhausted, drained, or being forced to walk.

12. Some people are so constipated that they feel lucky if they can move their bowels once every three to five days. Others have diarrhea at all times and may have to go to the toilet three to five times a day or after each meal.

13. Some people are so chilly they wear heavy clothes even during summer, making people wonder if they are sick. Other people are so hot they hardly wear any clothes, as if they want to expose themselves.

14. Some people snore so loudly that they wake up their neighbors. Others breathe so shallowly that they have to be checked to make sure they are breathing.

15. Some people drink so much water, it is as if there is fire in their body. Meanwhile, others don't drink water at all, as if they are doing a favor by leaving some for others.

16. At parties, some people overdress, making it hard to differentiate them from the groom/bride. Other people dress carelessly, as if they were not planning to come to the party.

17. Some people will do anything to lose a pound of weight, while others who will do anything to gain an ounce. Some people say they "look at food and get fat," while others eat like a horse and don't gain an ounce.

Mental level

1. Some people speak so loudly that their neighbors can hear them. They talk as if they are giving a speech or talking to a hundred people, but in reality, they are talking to only one person or even to themselves. (You must have observed that.) Others speak so softly that they need a microphone even for everyday conversations.

2. Some students study so much that even their parents have to tell them to enjoy life and relax—studying is not the only thing in life. Others don't study at all, to the point that even their friends and neighbors become concerned.

3. Some people talk incessantly without a break because they are afraid that if they stop, someone else will take over, and they will lose their chance to talk; others barely speak a sentence.

4. Some people are workaholics. Others want to be on welfare for the rest of their life, even when in the best of health—as if they are allergic to work.

5. Some people drive so fast, it feels like a comet has passed you or they are angry at you. Others drive slowly, as if they are lost.

6. Some people talk in your face to make sure that you smell their breath, while others talk at a distance, making you wonder if they are talking to you or to themselves.

7. Some people think so much they miss their flight, lose their things, and don't know where they left their belongings. Others don't think at all and need to hire help to think about minor daily decisions.

8. Some people love their children so much they spoil them, while other parents pay so little attention to their children that the children think something is wrong with them or their parents don't love them.

9. Some people own things and enjoy them at their will. Others are slaves to their things, neither using them for themselves, nor letting others use them.

10. Some bosses are so crazy that they give ulcers to their employees. The reverse can also be true; there are some crazy employees who give ulcers to their bosses.

11. Some people grieve over the loss of a sparrow, while others do not care for the suffering of humanity.

12. Some people will not open their purse for anything; others will spend so lavishly that they end up in bankruptcy.

Spiritual level

1. Some people have no concept of life even in the last days of life. Others take much interest in humanity, even during their early tender years.

2. Some people have so much faith (even blind faith), intense faith, that they pray several times a day and leave everything to God. Others have never seen the inside of a temple.

3. Some people believe in equal rights and respect the feelings of everyone. Others will do anything to control, rule, and abuse others; equal rights have no meaning to them.

4. Some people are not bothered by anything or any situation, while others jump out of their seat if somebody utters a wrong word.

Secret #13. Are you listening to your friendly guardian angels?

"I was awakened by a message from my guardian angels."
— Mrs. K.

You all must have experienced that, at difficult times when you are stressed, troubled or desperate for help, you get messages from the universe as if somebody "upstairs" or your guardian angels are watching you and want to help you. The reason is that the universe is your friend and you are part and parcel of it. I have an interesting story on this subject.

One day I was interviewing a new homeopathic patient, and as usual, I took a detailed history including a family history. (In homeopathic practice, it is important to understand the patient in totality. You can say that the physician must understand the patient not only from the diagnostic point of view, but also from other perspectives such as mental, spiritual, social, etc.)

While telling her story, she happened to mention that, "I am awakened by the message from my guardian angels that had changed my life."

I asked her, please explain to me what do you mean.

She continued, "It is very unfortunate that I come from a family where everybody is negative, depressed or miserable. One day I was meditating and I was feeling frustrated with the kind of life that I was living. Suddenly, I received a message from the guardian angel in the form of a faint voice speaking inside my head. It was very vivid. The message was, 'It is time for a change for a better and happier life. If you don't do it now, you will be the victim of sadness, depression, and misery like everybody else in the family.' I opened my eyes and there was nobody there. I closed my eyes again and I could no longer hear that voice. However, I realized that it was the voice of my guardian angel and therefore, I decided that it is the time to make a change, and so I did.

"Immediately thereafter, I decided that I must take the initiative for change, otherwise I would be the victim of my own behavior and I would also be guilty of passing this behavior down to my children, as my parents had done to me. This incident has turned around my life. Today I am happy and proud of the change that I have made in my life.

"To me, it was a wake-up call from my guardian angel, or you can call it God."

Next, let me share another story in this context that happened to me personally. It was about twelve years ago, and I was facing some problems: not one, but three.

I was sad and disappointed, which is not typical of me, because I am an optimistic person. One morning when driving my car to work, all of a sudden, my car slowed down to the point that I felt it was going to stop. I also felt sleepy. Suddenly, I woke up and saw two hands in front of my face. These two hands gave me a message of assurance and told me not to worry and everything would be fine. Believe it or not, my first problem was solved on the very first day and the other two problems also got resolved, but took a little more time. I realized it was a message from the guardian angel, or the universe.

I think that your friendly guardian angels are up there watching and protecting you, especially when you are lost and clueless. They are there for you in your time of need. So, keep tuned to them. However, for proper tuning you need to relax. I believe it is much easier to connect with them especially if you are a relaxed person and/or practice relaxation or meditation.

If you ask me how many guardian angels are up there, I would say nobody has an answer for that. However, I do believe that there are plenty of them for every human being, therefore we do not have to worry about that part.

The key message- there is 'Hope' for everyone.

Secret #14. How partial information can hurt you?

The "AHA" moment.

In life, people suffer at times just because they make judgments or conclusions based upon incomplete or partial information available to them, without knowing or understanding all the facts. Let me clarify this through an interesting story of a patient.

A 53-year-old lady came to see me because she was sad and felt neglected by her boss. She also had an element of jealousy and anger. I listened to her story in detail, and I am presenting you the story in the patient's own language. I am sure when you use your analytical mind, you will be able to appreciate where the problem lies.

The patient said, "I have been a restaurant manager for 20 years, working for the same boss and for the same restaurant. My boss's business had been flourishing and he had opened another restaurant and hired a young girl with a college degree to manage it. Before opening this new restaurant, my boss used to come to the restaurant where I worked, and we had a friendly relationship and he was good to me. Since he has opened the new restaurant, he does not come to this one anymore. Most of the time he is at the new restaurant where the young girl is the manager. I feel neglected and forsaken. I'm angry at the boss and at the new manager. I am sad and have difficulty sleeping. I feel hurt. I do not understand why my boss is treating me like this after 20 years."

After listening to the story, I asked her to tell me if she was a good manager. She replied, "Yes, my boss used to say that you're so good a manager that you don't need my help. I remember that one time my boss also told me 'If you could manage this place by yourself, then I can open another restaurant.'"

(This statement from the patient gave me great insight into the situation.)

I told her, "What I think is that you are such a good manager that your boss does not think that you need his help."

After she heard my opinion, she started to smile and asked, "Do you think that is the case?"

I told her, "I don't know, but you will find out."

I suggested that she should ask her boss why he does not come to her restaurant anymore. After a month, she came back and told me, "Doctor, you were right. My boss said to me exactly what you have told me. He repeated once again, that if you can find another good manager like you, I can open even a third restaurant." She let out a sigh of relief and before leaving she said, "Why I did not think of that before? Thank you very much for the insight. Now I feel happy and proud of my work and myself."

Partial information can be very misleading and can be the cause of many problems including sadness, misunderstanding, disagreement and of course unhappiness. So, the wise often say, never judge or conclude anything without understanding all the facts. It can save you from many miseries.

Secret #15. Conscience and happiness — the important link!

I am a happy person because I listen to my soul
— Mrs. K

Most likely you are aware of the fact that people who are guided by their conscience are much happier than those who are guided by other elements such as emotions, material possessions, self-interest, etc. You may also know that the soul equates to the consciousness, and it is the innermost and most essential element of life.

Here is the story of Mr. and Mrs. K, who has been my patient for more than two years. They live from hand to mouth and at times cannot even afford her costly medicine. Mrs. K is one of the greatest people I know, and always has a happy demeanor. One day I asked her, "Mrs. K, you live in such desperate straits, please tell me, what is the secret of your happiness?"

She replied, "I am a happy person because I listen to my soul."

I asked her, "Please tell me more, how it applies to your life."

She continued, "I have seen very tough times in my life financially and at times even with my family. But

I have never given into the wrongful path. I always did whatever was right for me and the family. That has helped me a lot. Although we are poor, we are a happy family and I am proud of that. It is all because I listen to my conscience and work accordingly."

Mr. Gerry Spence, the author of the book *How to Argue and Win Every Time, at Home, at Work, in the Court and Everywhere,* has stated something similar. When he wrote, "You can give everything to your wife, but don't give in to your principles," I think he was trying to convey the same message.

The conscience and happiness are deeply linked with each other. One cannot exist without the other. You know that conscience is the highest element of human life. Therefore, it becomes important to listen to one's conscience while making important decisions in life. It is hard to go wrong when you do that.

A person who works with his or her conscience will find happiness in the long run, although at times he or she may have to deal with some difficult times/challenges. In contrast, when people work against their conscience, not only can it cause damage to their soul, but when they come to the realization that they have been treading the wrong path, it can be often too late.

Secret #16. Intentions versus outcome: who wins?

Intentions and actions are usually directly related. However, sometimes things don't happen as planned, and in that case, intentions get the points versus the actions. Let me share a story that exemplifies the above point.

Our family was on vacation and we were at the hotel pool. The weather was hot and many families were having fun there. The people were throwing balls at each other. Accidentally one of the balls hit my son's head. Suddenly, my attention went first to my son and then to the person who hit the ball.

The person looked at me and said, "I am very sorry. I could not hit your son even if I wanted to." Thereafter he never looked back again. Why? Because he knew he was not guilty, and of course he did not mean to hit my son. He also knew in his heart that I would accept his apology. So, he was confident and clear in his conscience.

Intentions are extremely powerful, and often can override the outcome.

Secret #17. Why is everybody just a number in this vast universe?

In this vast world, there are people of all calibers from lowest to highest, yet everybody is just a number. Why?

Firstly, the universe is so vast that it is hard to comprehend even to the greatest scientist. Just think that on the Earth where we live, there are seven billion people, at the time of writing. Some are so smart that one even cannot comprehend, and it can make one dizzy. Secondly, the earth itself is just a small speck in this universe which consists of billions of galaxies. Lastly, we know that everything in this world is temporary, that includes name, fame, money, position, power and so on. Therefore, if anybody thinks he is a great and indispensable person, it is a mistake. The person lives in a delusional state.

In this world, nobody stands even a chance to be great, at least not for long. Therefore, one must get rid of ego. Because the ego is the root cause of unhappiness and unease, whereas humility is the cause of happiness and ease. This is one of the real secrets of a happy life.

I shall discuss two stories to make my point.

One of my relatives and a doctor friend came from India and stayed with us for three days. He is a neurologist and the purpose of his visit was to present a paper to the International Association of Neurologists.

On his third day with us, it happened to be Sunday. My wife and I were working in the yard and he came to help us. I told him, "You do not need to help us, you are a guest."

He replied "If I am staying with the family, I also must contribute something to the family." After hearing his statement, I looked at him with a feeling of admiration and then I nodded my head in acceptance.

Three years ago, I visited India. It was a fun trip, and 10 days long. My wife and my sister-in-law were with me. In India, hospitality is the rule rather than the exception. We were all fed well and taken care of. During our visit, we met lots of friends and family because I come from a big family. Thus, we all gained weight, and of course, we all had good times.

I visited one of my sisters. She lives in a joint family with his son, his wife and the grandson. As soon as we arrived, all the family members gathered around us to welcome us and to show their affection. At dinner time, they served a five-course meal. Before we began to eat, my sister's son, Rajinder, said something beautiful to express his feelings: "Dr. Singhal, we are honored to have you as a guest. Please accept this simple food that we have prepared for you."

I was touched by his statement. I looked deep into his eyes in admiration and appreciation. He bowed his head out of humility. Then I told him, "Dear Rajinder, of course, I would like to thank you for your hospitality, but today is the day that I have come to realize how kind and humble a person you are."

Rajinder is a lovely man with a religious background. He does not eat his breakfast till he does his prayers and rituals. He is an extremely kind and affectionate person, not only to his family but to his clients who come to his small factory. He is an extremely happy man.

Ego and humility are two sides of the same coin. Ego is a sign of immaturity, whereas humility is a sign of maturity and wisdom.

I have stated in my earlier writings that the person who thinks that he or she is somebody is nobody, and is a victim of ego or ignorance. However, a person who come to realize the fact that he is nobody is mature and wise. That wise person is not only happy and at ease within themselves but also bestows the same upon others.

Secret #18. How deep faith in God and the self helps some people to go through tough times?

From my years of experience, I have come to believe that faith in God and/or the self can be very rewarding for one's mental stability and of course happiness. I shall narrate two short stories to make my point.

As you know, God is an abstract element; that is why some people believe in him while others don't. However, I can say from personal experience that people who believe in Him usually are much happier. Of course, there is no denying that there are many happy people who do not believe in God. Here is the first story about the power of the belief in God.

I had known Mrs. J for only one year. She had quite a large share of financial troubles. Recently her husband had lost his job and they had received a notice of eviction from her apartment. She came to see me for some medical issue and she was pregnant. She was pleasant and had a good demeanor even under the circumstances. I was surprised by her behavior, knowing the background information. I asked her "How are you keeping your mental balance under the circumstances?"

She replied, "I know my God will take care of me and He has done it before." She further said "Worse comes to worst, I will find another place of lesser value and lesser quality. But I am happy because my family is together and my husband and I love each other very much."

Later, I learned that she was not evicted for a period of two years.

Here is another story of this type. One of my good friends and a devotee of God had one trouble after another, but he kept himself calm and composed during all the difficult times. He used to say, "God knows me well, and he also knows how much I can handle. He will not give me more than I can handle. God is just testing me."

You can appreciate from these two stories how faith in God and the self can be a cause of inner strength and courage that can help a person to go through tough times in life.

Secret #19. Awakening!

This story is about a young couple who got married recently. The wife was a most beautiful woman and her husband was deeply in love with her. You could say he was crazy about her. His wife was in deep love with him also. She was not only beautiful but also a very religious person, a devotee of God, and used to pray a lot. On the other hand, the husband had no love or regard for God. You could say he was neutral on the subject, though as a matter of fact he did not believe in God.

Once the wife decided to visit her parents for a week. The husband became sad in her absence and decided to visit her. The day he decided to travel was stormy and very rainy. It was a long journey of one full night. When he arrived at his in-law's house, he received a proper welcome and was very pleased. However, at night when his wife came to sleep with him, she said to him, "I know you love me very much and I love you too. But coming here in the stormy and rainy night, it does not look as good." She further stated, "If you would love God, even half as much as you love me, God will be pleased with you."

This statement from his wife shocked him and his soul was awakened. This incident changed his life. In the morning, he left his in-laws and became a devotee of God. Thereafter he enjoyed real peace in life and started to enjoy greater happiness and contentment. Thereafter, he became closer to his wife also and understood her feeling and her love for God.

The message of the story is that awakening can change one's life in a flash. Many stories in this book have the purpose of awakening or self-arousal.

Secret #20. The present time is too precious to waste on past issues!

It is the real-life story of a teacher who was wrongly accused of something in school. He defended himself successfully, and all the charges were dismissed. The judge also declared that all the accusations were wrong. Thereafter he resigned from his school and started his own small company.

Many people told him that he should not let go of these people. "They deserve punishment and you must sue them for the damages that they have caused you. Now you have a solid proof that you were accused wrongly."

He replied, "I am through with the school and with the school life. I wish to move on with my new life. I don't want to waste my money, energy and my precious time on getting revenge or compensation. I know I can win. But I would rather have peace at heart and save precious moments of my life, rather than wasting it on revengeful actions."

Rehashing the past usually means wasting time and energy with little or no benefit, and it can become a long, draining affair. Thus, wise people tell us to forget the past and focus on making the future. One also need to remember that the past is gone, nobody knows the future, and the only handle you have is on the present. Love it. Take advantage of it to its maximum. It is equally true that the past is what was the present at one time, and of course the future has its root in the present. In other words, the present is the basis of all times, past as well as future.

I further believe, when one lives in the past, it is hard to move in the future, because the past becomes the roadblock.

Secret # 21. The 'joy and Blues' of holidays?

Here is a little learning experience I had. Once I wished a patient "Happy Holidays" during the Christmas season.

She replied, "Doctor, please do not mention the word holidays to me, because it brings sadness and tears."

I asked her why. She replied "Because it was at Christmastime, 11 years ago, that my mother died, and she was very close to me."

This was the first time that I came to the realization that holidays can be a cause of sadness to some people, and after this incident, I understood that this patient was not the only one. Thereafter, I met a few other patients, who also fell into this category. Anyhow, I advised my patient that she should remember and celebrate her mother's birthday and try not to focus on the day she died. Because the birthday brings good memories and has positive connotations.

We need to focus on something positive, such as birthdays, anniversaries, graduations or any good memories as it gives us uplift. However, when one focuses on the negative it can be a cause of sadness and depression. This is one of the reasons that we celebrate the birthdays of great people like Mahatma Gandhi, George Washington, Martin

Luther King, Lord Krishna, Lord Rama and so on. Nobody ever celebrates the day a person dies.

In essence, holidays can mean different things to different people, and may have positive or even negative connotations. That is the reason there is a common phrase, "holiday joy and holiday blues."

Secret #22. When loss or win has no meaning!

Winning has different meanings to different people. It is also true that at times, it can become difficult to differentiate between a win and a loss. For now, just read on:

One day I was playing an indoor game in bed with my seven-year-old son. It was a very cold, wintry night. Somehow, I lost the game. Immediately thereafter my son started to jump for joy, and kept jumping for two minutes, and kept repeating the statement that, "I have beaten Daddy, I have beaten Daddy." On that day, I had so much more fun in losing and seeing the excitement of my son than I ever had in winning.

From then on, I have used this technique of losing several times while playing with other children, and it works. This experience has strengthened my belief that when you make others happy, it adds to your own happiness. The nearer and dearer the person, the happier you feel.

Allow me to cite a little story from one of the epics of India, known as a Ramayana. This is the story of a great king who became a symbol of worship for thousands of years to come. The King's name was Rama. During his childhood, he used to play the same technique with his little brother Baharat. Rama used to lose to his little brother just to make him happy. Both brothers were in great love with each other. This love continued even when Rama became the King.

Last weekend, when our family was on vacation, two of my grandchildren were playing air hockey and I was watching the game. The children are twins, eight years old. My grandson was winning the game over his twin sister by a wide margin. Suddenly, he realized that his sister was getting sad. Thereafter, he played a smart trick, to make her happy. He started to lose intentionally till they were equal. Then he told her twin sister, "Look, we are equal — I'm not winning."

My heart was filled with love for my grandson, what a big heart an eight-year-old boy can have!

When something make you feel happy in your heart and soul, the loss or the win, loses its meaning. In olden days, people lived with the philosophy of winning or losing. However, in the modern age, everybody wants to create a win-win situation. This is in a way keeping up with this philosophy.

Secret #23. How a wise old man met death's challenge (an example of courage and wisdom)

Have you ever given a thought to what goes through a person's mind when he is told he has a short time to live?

Mr. JH was 85 years old and had been my patient for many years. He was blind, but a very wise man and had a deep understanding of life. On his last admission to the hospital, he was diagnosed with kidney failure and dialysis was his only hope. When I offered him the choice, he refused?

I asked him why he was refusing the treatment and he replied, "Dr. Singhal, my roommate has the same problem as I have. I see how much he is suffering. He goes to dialysis three times a week, and after every treatment, he feels bad for a day. By the time he recovers, he is ready for the next treatment."

Mr. JH continued; he said, "Dr. Singhal, please listen to me, nobody lives forever and everybody must die one day. I would rather die with dignity and peace rather than be the victim of the side effects of dialysis and suffer. To me, quality of life is more important than just surviving. I understand that dialysis will just prolong my life for some time, and to me that is not living."

After hearing his reasoning, I became quiet. I had nothing more to offer to him. Therefore, I had no choice except to agree with his decision not to be treated, and he was transferred to a long-term nursing home care facility. I visited him on a daily basis, so that I could keep an eye on him in case he changed his mind and/or if I could be of any help in his last days.

From that day on, he stopped eating and drinking. He also closed his eyes for good. He never moved or spoke thereafter. The only time he spoke was if I asked him questions. On each visit, he would answer only three questions and no more. His answers were brief. Here is the typical dialogue between him and me, in the final days of his life.

Dr.: Mr. JH, how are you?

Mr. JH: I am fine.

Dr.: Do you need something?

Mr. JH: No.

Dr.: Can I not do something for you?

Mr. JH: No.

If I would ask him any other question, he would say, "It is not important, so I choose not to answer."

This pattern of dialogue continued till the last day of his life. He was as calm as anybody could be, until the last day. I observed that he died peacefully with respect and dignity, per his wish. And when I attended his funeral, calmness was written across his face.

It requires wisdom and courage to say, enough is enough. Or to choose quality of life versus just living a little longer.

You must agree that many people in their lives may have to face this difficult and challenging decision, when and if they are diagnosed with a terminal illness. Then the same question will arise in the mind of the person or even the family, whether to choose quality or quantity of life. Whether to prolong life while sacrificing the joy of living, or just quit and die with peace and dignity. On several occasions, I have observed that many wise people choose not to suffer unnecessarily. It is the fruit of wisdom. I bear a deep regard for them.

Secret #24. When death knocks at the door, how does a patient respond?

Everybody knows that death is the most natural and inevitable phenomenon of life, that everybody has to face one day. However, it requires a lot of courage and wisdom to accept that.

It was one of the saddest days of my life when I learned that my brother-in-law was on his deathbed. He was in India and I was in the USA. I phoned him immediately and got to chat with him for a few minutes. I just listened and let him talk most of the time. He spoke in a weak voice, but with great clarity. During the conversation, he made a very a powerful statement that I will share with you.

He said in a tone of contentment: "I'm ready when God is ready for me. I had a good life."

Much has been written about death. But I do not think anybody knows all the facts about it. However, two things are certain. Firstly, nobody can escape from it; secondly, nobody knows when it is going to come.

Death is a scary thing for most people. However, it requires courage to understand and accept death as a natural phenomenon that everybody has to face one day. Accepting death as a natural phenomenon can be challenging but rewarding. Because once a person accepts it, the person will have no problem breaking away all the bonds with the family and dear ones that he/she has created. That means a peaceful death, and a great reward.

The definition of death varies from culture to culture and religion to religion. Some people believe that death is the end of life, whereas many religions (especially Hinduism) believe in a life continuum that includes rebirth and so on.

Secret #25. Which is the single most precious gift of all?

Mrs. WM is a 90-year-old lady and has been my patient for 15 years. She comes to my office periodically for a checkup. She had a great emotional setback after the death of her husband. She has been in need of assurance from time to time, but otherwise, she has been okay. She has her share of medical issues, which is not unusual for this age group. However, she is quite a wise lady and often makes valuable remarks. One time she said something beautiful that I will quote here for you.

She said, "Life is the most precious gift of all — you better enjoy it."

Although this statement is very simple, there is a powerful truth behind it. The important fact is that when a person can understand this in their heart and soul, and practice it in daily life, it can have a significant impact on his or her life.

Secret #26. You are not the problem!

The purpose of this section is to make clear to everyone that you and your problems are two different elements. Problems are part of everybody's life, and you are not the problem. You are a problem-solver.

It is very sad when people associate themselves with a problem, or think they are the cause of the problem. It is not true. It is an error on their part. It is like the way some people associate themselves with their belongings such as clothes, houses, cars and so on, yet their belongings are not them.

You need to remember that you are here for a long, wonderful journey of life, whereas your problems are like little black clouds that come and go. At times these clouds might thunder or even rain, but quite often they disappear without leaving any effect, leaving you as the sun, shining behind those black clouds.

The key is that one must learn to differentiate oneself from problems. This approach has many advantages, for example you stay calm, you see solutions with clarity, and most importantly, you understand that you are not the problem.

There are several techniques of dissociation, some of which are healthy, whereas others are not. Some examples of healthy dissociation are meditation, prayer, directing the mind to a good cause, or just simply taking a pause. Of course, you must remember that, eventually you do have to solve the problem once you're feeling calm and strong.

On the other hand, some examples of unhealthy dissociation would be drugs, alcohol, etc. These are things you never want to let into your life. Because these have long-term negative consequences.

Here are some examples. Let us begin with a person who dissociates him or herself from a problem by saying, "I cannot think about this problem now, I am busy with something more important than this and I will deal with it later when I have time for it." What a powerful technique!

Let me give you one more example: a person who, whenever he has a problem, says, "God is testing me again, but I will go through."

Mrs. CT has been my patient for three years. She has also been facing poverty for a while. Things are so bad that at times the only meal the family gets is bread and tea. On many occasions, she has trouble making payment for her office visits, but she will usually say, "Do not worry, Doctor, you will get paid eventually," and I trust her. She is a very content and happy person and is very appreciative of everything, including the medical treatment that I give her.

One day I asked her how she maintains her attitude of contentment in such a difficult time. She replied, "Poverty does not mean misery. I am doing my best under the circumstances. I take one day at a time. I do not tend to think of tomorrow. And I'm doing just fine."

I wish to draw your attention to the most important part of that statement: I take one day at a time; I do not like to think of tomorrow. By doing so she is trying to dissociate herself from the problems of tomorrow.

This technique of dissociating oneself from problems is a wonderful one which puts you in charge of the situation. I like to quote from a well-known reverend who has stated, "Tough people last, but tough times don't." What a powerful and positive message! This technique of dissociation can be used in many situations related to work, children, parental issues, family issues, divorce, financial issues, and so on.

Secret #27. My experience of working at a psychiatric hospital for one week.

Once I had the opportunity to work at a psychiatric hospital for one week as a medical doctor. I realized quickly how hard it was to work with psychiatric patients. Most of the patients were okay with me, and that is not the point of discussion. But I was struck by the lives of few psychiatric patients. Let me give you some examples:

Quite a few of patients had tried to commit suicide, some out of frustration and others out of depression. During the week I was on call, I examined one patient who had jumped from the third floor because he saw a dog on the road and he thought the dog was going to attack him.

Several of the patients were extremely restless, walking day and night on the floor at a fast pace. I felt helpless and could not understand what kind of pain and anguish these patients must be going through. I also noticed that some patients were constantly yelling and screaming, so loud that their voices could be heard on the next floor.

After one week on call, I told the director of the psychiatric ward that this job was not for me. I also asked him to tell me how he kept his own sanity under the circumstances. In response, he said something truly beautiful: "Dr. Singhal, I count my blessings."

The purpose of this story is to impress upon you that work has so many rewards of its own that it often overrides the occupational hazards associated with it. People need work not only to get a paycheck only but because it provides a sense of fulfillment which is good for self-worth and gives energy that makes life worthwhile. That is one of the reasons there are so many workaholics. Further, without work, one's mind becomes the devil's workshop.

Secret #28. When 'Happiness' has to go in search of happy people?

Once I was visiting one of my friends and we were having a cup of tea and chit-chatting. My attention went to his wife who was watering the plants. What amazed me was that as she was watering the plants she was smiling, talking and touching them as if they could understand her. She was also looking at the plants with deep love. I could not resist asking her about this. I said to Mrs. PW, "I see you have a lot of love for these plants. You are smiling, talking and touching them as you water them."

She replied with a smile, "Yes, of course. We have no children. To me, these plants are my children. I enjoy seeing them grow. I also believe these plants miss me and love me very much as if I am their mother."

'Happiness' needs happy people as much as people need 'happiness.' When people are busy in their happy life, happiness has to go find them, or else she cannot survive. In other words, happy people do not have to search for happiness, it comes to them.

Secret #29. Adaptability and flexibility, the two amazing secrets of happiness!

We are told by wise people that adaptability or flexibility is an integral ingredient of a happier life, whereas rigidity (or being unable to adapt) can be a cause of unhappiness or even misery. Here is an instructional story about this.

It was one of the very cold days in December when my CPA came to see me at my home for accounting purposes. So, it was a business meeting. I asked him "Would you like to have a cup of tea, because it is so cold outside?"

He replied, "Yes, only if you are having it, otherwise there is no need to make it for me."

I was amazed by his statement, which was so simple but sent a powerful message. I was expecting him to say, "Sure, it is cold outside." Secondly, what impressed me most was the second part of the statement, i.e. "I don't have to have it, or I am not counting on it'.

His last statement that I don't have to have it, or I am not counting on it. Keep me thinking for a long time to come. I have learned a lot from that statement. I learned how flexibility can add to happiness.

Secret #30. Tolerance and acceptance — a tribute!

Tolerance and acceptance are some of the important causes of happiness. It has nothing to do with education, college degrees, social status or anything else.

I have witnessed the lives of several servants as they came to serve my parents. I realized that although most of them were uneducated, most if not all were happy and content in their personal lives. They were not touched or hurt easily by criticism or the annoyances of daily life. Most of them were happy that they had a job to earn a living. To them, that was worth a lot. Most of them had strong tolerance as if that went with that kind of job.

Once we had a servant from Nepal. He was a Vedic scholar and a wise man. He had a happy demeanor and was very hard-working. I never saw him sitting down. He was always doing something or the other as if it was his own house. After retiring at night, he would go to his room and study Vedas (the book of knowledge, the Hindu scriptures) that he had borrowed from my brother. He told me that sometimes he studied the scriptures till two or three o'clock in the morning.

What impressed me most was, if and when somebody said something to him which he did not like, he would just smile and get busy with his work, without saying anything. I had never seen him grumbling or angry. In other words, he would wash off all the negativity with a smile. That was his technique.

At that time, I was 14 years old and became close friends with him. I learned a lot from him about his attitude towards work and how he took criticism yet maintained his happy demeanor.

Tolerance and acceptance are very strong elements to happiness. It may come naturally when one has to do a menial job, but for most people it comes with maturity and wisdom.

Secret #31. Acceptance/gratitude!

The story is a recent one. One of my medical colleagues was making rounds in the hospital. All of a sudden, his face got red and he passed out. There was no warning, because when he arrived that morning in the hospital, he was feeling perfectly normal.

At the time of this incident his blood pressure was elevated to 220/110. Fortunately, one of his colleagues was with him at the time. He took my friend immediately to the emergency department of the hospital. A CAT scan of his head was done and it revealed internal bleeding into the brain. He was immediately transferred to a bigger hospital affiliated with this hospital. The neurosurgeon was standing by. As soon as my doctor friend arrived, the neurosurgeon drilled a hole in the top of his head and drained lot of blood from his brain. That saved my doctor friend's life. In a matter of four to five months, my friend had totally recovered.

When I met him after his recovery, he told me something very interesting. He said that his father used to say to him that, we need to live with the philosophy that we are given a life of 50 years, and thereafter all is extra. You enjoy it, and thank God every day for that. By the way, my friend is a devotee of God. I want you to appreciate how the element of contentment/gratitude can provide all the joy in life.

Secret #32. Contentment!

There is a Christian mission located not far from my office. Quite a few people from the mission are my patients. They are quite calm, caring and gentle people, and not very demanding. What has colored their life may not be as much their religion as the fact that their life is devoted to helping people, and that is what they live for. They are not paid well and luxury is not part of their lives.

Two of those patients from the mission told me that according to the Bible, human life is supposed to be around 60 or so years, and thereafter it is all extra. (Although I do not agree with them personally on the statement, that is not the point of discussion here.) The fact that I want to bring to your attention is that they are very content with their lives. This element of contentment is one of the greatest gifts and a cause of joy and happiness. This is also one of my life's observations.

Secret #33. What comes around, goes around — a bona fide truth!

I bring this story to you because it has a powerful message. One of my doctor friends used this phrase quite often. Eventually, I began to understand the implication and the power of the phrase.

Dr. R was a good friend of mine; we worked together for many years in the same hospital. I was quite impressed with one of his behaviors. He would never say anything bad or negative to anyone.

Let me share an example: One day I was sitting with him in the cafeteria and we were having breakfast together. When the chief of the surgical team came in, he was saying nasty things to everyone. The chief seemed to be upset about something. My friend looked at him for a moment, and then turned his head down and mumbled, "What comes around goes around." Thereafter he continued his breakfast, and we continued our conversation and to laugh for some time.

It is like the teaching of Buddha: if you don't accept what others are giving to you, it goes back to the person who wants to give it to you.

This is a great phrase, and the practical one. Of course, every great human being has his or her own unique way of dealing with negative situations and challenges.

Secret #34. Should you ever retire? A big question

One of my favorite statements is, retirement is for those who wish to retire from life. (It may be too broad a statement, and you do not have to agree with it in totality.)

Once I had the opportunity to listen to a great psychiatrist friend speak. His clear-cut message was that one should not retire. Ever since, this message has stuck with me and I see its importance. Therefore, I have been sharing this message with many of my patients, friends, and families. Here I have the opportunity to share it with you.

I have been observing that after retirement, many people deteriorate rapidly or even die, as if they have lost their purpose in life. When people ask me, "Dr. Singhal, when will you retire?" I often reply, only when God will make me. I personally have no plans for retirement. I believe that one should retire only when he or she wants to retire from life.

In our modern culture, people are in the habit of using the word happy as a prefix to many things, for example, happy birthday, happy anniversary, happy holidays, happy Christmas, happy Valentine's Day, etc. Nowadays people have even started to say happy retirement. Let me say a word about the definition of retirement. To some people, retirement means that they have put in enough hours of work in their lifetime and now it is time to rest (or even rust, if you so like to call it).

And you know, too much rest can rust a person, because it is not good for the body, mind or the soul. This kind of retirement can have bad consequences.

However, if your plan is to keep busy with something purposeful after retiring, for example finding another job, pursuing a hobby, getting involved with some social or community project, etc., that is great and healthy for the body and mind. To me, this may be the only time when you can call it a happy retirement.

From my own experience and that of many wise people, I have come to understand that life is action and without action there is no life. If I had to summarize the whole message in four words I would say,

"Say no to retirement."

Secret # 35. Too-busy life, a curse or a blessing?

A busy life may be good, but a too-busy life, I'm not so sure?

In life nothing is 100 percent good or bad. This is definitely true of the busy life; it has both a positive and a negative side. Since the busy life has so many rewards, such as the sense of accomplishment, pride and so on, some people often get blinded to the negative side of it.

Let me cite you two examples: The first is the story of a millionaire who is a single parent. He got rich through hard work and not by sitting at home. He travels, tours and is busy with meetings and in whatever time is left, he is at his desk finalizing and reviewing documents. Since his focus has been money, he has earned a lot of it.

His wife has left him because she never saw him at home. He has only one son who does not see his daddy and is being taken care of by maids and servants. You all know that the maids and the servants cannot replace the parents. The worst part is that the millionaire has lost insight into his situation. He cannot understand why his wife has left him although he was one of the best providers. She could buy anything that she wanted to, but that was not what she wanted, and he could not understand that. Now it is a similar situation with his son. His mind is so busy with business and money that he cannot comprehend that money is not everything.

Let me give you another example. I have an older couple who are my patients and are in their late seventies. They have nine children, 14 grandchildren, and three great-grandchildren. When I see this couple in my office, they complain they are tired, and they look tired. I asked them how much sleep they got and they replied, "Maybe four to five hours." Next, I asked, why are you not getting enough sleep? They replied, "Because we are too busy babysitting grandchildren or at times even great-grandchildren. So, we do not have enough time to rest."

I asked them, why don't you tell your children? This was their reply: They raised the issue with one child, who is an executive and makes good money. He replied, "Dad, I am very busy right now; let me make some money for just a few more years, and thereafter you can take it easy." But the statement of "just a few more years" is going on and on with no end in sight.

They raised the same concern with the second son. He just laughed and said, "My dear parents, my son needs the love of his grandparents." Next, they asked the third son, and he was kind of rude and said, "Don't you love your grandchildren?" When they asked the fourth son, he just smiled and left in a hurry. He said that he would talk about it a little later. But later has not come yet.

Children often cannot, or do not wish to understand the helplessness or the stress of their parents. And parents are in no position to keep pressing their children and cannot say no to them. It is a sensitive issue. This is the effect of the too-busy life where everybody is suffering and nobody knows an easy solution, or how to get out of the cycle.

My patients, the couple, are not only suffering physically but also emotionally. They are caught in a Catch-22. Although there are many positive and negative aspects of a busy life, the most unfortunate part is that it makes people forget to relax and reflect on the real purpose for which life has been granted.

Secret #36. How big is your heart? Can you measure it?

Does a big heart have any connection with happiness? Yes, it does. But before going into the subject, I must clarify what is meant by big heart, otherwise this can lead to confusion. The phrase has two connotations, one positive and the other negative.

In medical terms, when a doctor says such-and-such person has a big heart, it means the person has a diseased heart and it is a warning sign. Conversely, in English literature or in the emotional language, it has a positive connotation. It means the person is forgiving, generous, caring, loving, open-minded and so on.

So, if you ever meet a person with a big heart (emotionally speaking), stay with them, shadow them, love them. You can recognize these people from a distance. They attract other people as honey attracts flies. If you stay with them long enough, they will color your life for the better. It will bring a lot of happiness into your life. Please be aware that this element of a big heart can be quite contagious and these qualities of theirs will rub off on you. Ultimately, you will thank them and thank yourself for being part of their friendship.

Now you know how to measure the size of anybody's heart, emotionally speaking.

Secret #37. Stress: the necessary evil?

The purpose of the following section is threefold. Firstly, to show you that stress is a necessity for growth and development. Secondly, that stress does not affect everybody equally, and finally, to show what can be done to solve the issue of stress.

Firstly, I believe stress is a necessity. I cannot imagine a successful life without it. You all know that life is full of stresses from birth until death. Just look at some of the following examples: birth (coming to a new and strange world), going to kindergarten (separation from parents), adolescence (becoming independent and detaching from parents), higher education (learning new skills and gaining knowledge), marriage (dealing with a new partner who may have totally different values), job (the challenges of the work, boss and coworkers), pregnancy (preparing for the new one), dealing with family and relatives, sicknesses and finally death.

Secondly, you all know that stress does not affect everybody equally. With the same degree of stress some people get sad, burn out, get depressed or even kill themselves, while others grow stronger and stronger while dealing with challenges successfully. Don't you want to belong to this latter category of people? (You know the statement that what does not kill you makes you stronger.)

There are two factors that will determine how stress will affect a person: How strong is the stress? How strong is the person?

The stronger a person is, the less likely he/she is to be affected by stress. Of course, it is also true that stronger stress will affect more people, and conversely, weaker stress will affect fewer people. Let me give you a concrete example. You all know how bad 9/11 was. In that incident, roughly 3000 people died in a flash. But did this tragedy affect everyone equally? Of course not.

Some of my neighbors were a family of four — the husband, the wife, and two children. The husband was killed on 9/11. But the wife was strong. She bounced back quickly and has returned to normal life. It was a thing of pride, for the family and for others who were related to them.

Whereas after 9/11, I had to treat many patients who suffered emotionally, and whose symptoms included loss of sleep, fear and anger. And none of them were directly or indirectly involved in the incident, yet some of them suffered because to my understanding they were not strong enough emotionally for such stress.

Thirdly, let me discuss how to deal with stress from my own experience. I think there are two possible ways and they are complementary to each other.

The first solution is, that one needs to be strong physically as well as mentally. Because you all know that stronger people are not easily affected by stress, or as a matter of fact by anything else. Yoga and meditation offer great hope for them. Of course, there are other modalities as well, such as exercise, healthy diet and so on.

And the second solution is, to take a short pause or little break. Next, reflect or think how you can deal with the stress. However, one cannot forget that one had to deal with it in the end, or else it can haunt you for a long time. Why is a pause or delay important? Because the little pause or extra time provides an opportunity to look into the situation more calmly and with more clarity. And secondly, with the passage of time everything decreases in strength and importance.

I have a doctor friend who used to say that whenever he got a letter which stressed him, he would not look at it again until 24 hours later. This gave him the time to assimilate the information. After 24 hours, he would look at the letter again. At this juncture, if he still felt that he could not see the solution or was feeling stressed, he closed the letter again until the following day. He said it was his experience that when he opened the letter with a calm mind when he could see the solution, and it was very relieving, in contrast to the problem, which was stressing him.

In conclusion, I must say that stress is important for growth and development. Therefore, I firmly believe that one should never make a mountain of it, rather one should face it with intelligence and wisdom. I will even say one should embrace it.

Secret #38. How to take advantage of a catalyst?

First, let me clarify what a catalyst is. The Oxford English Dictionary has two definitions of a catalyst. However, I am giving you the one which is applicable to this writing. The catalyst is a substance that increases the rate of reaction without itself undergoing any permanent change.

Now let me give you two good examples of how a catalyst plays an important role in life. The first example is any game where the cheerleaders and the fans of a team act as a catalyst and help the team to win the game, by boosting their confidence.

The second example is from my personal experience. During my childhood, when and if I ever got sad or felt low, my parents used to say, "Pratap, your name is a symbol of bravery and you cannot let the little silly things of life bring you down." That statement has helped to uplift me on several occasions. The encouraging words of my parents are another example of a catalyst.

How can you use a catalyst to your benefit? In your life, you must have some people who have always been a source of encouragement, inspiration, and uplift to you. These might be your parents, your teachers, friends, peers, neighbors or someone else. At those times when you feel down or have bad days, remember those people and their words and you will find them uplifting. In this scenario, those people or their words would be a catalyst for you.

If you so choose, you may also use this book as a catalyst, if you let it.

Secret #39. How to benefit from anchoring?

You need to know that anchoring is a powerful tool that anybody can use in tough or bad times, especially when you need a little lift, push, or encouragement. Good days, good memories and good moments can help you in bad times, and therefore can be used as an anchor.

This is how it can be done. Firstly, I suggest you make a list of the best days, best memories, and the best moments of your life that have helped to uplift your spirits in the past and make you feel good. These may be the day of graduation, a promotion, becoming a parent, or the day you received an award or were recognized for something. You should read this list often. And every time you read this list you should touch your right thumb and vice versa. In other words, whenever you will touch your right thumb you would remember that list. Now your right thumb has become your anchor.

In the 2nd step, whenever you feel down or sad, touch your right thumb again. This should remind you of your good days and memories that have been uplifting for you in the past. You will find this will ease your pain and will boost your energy level, and may even provide some guidance. This is called the technique of anchoring.

You can use this technique for many other purposes also, for example getting rid of bad habits such as smoking or laziness, or acquiring healthy habits.

Secret #40. 'Needs and wants', and the ongoing war between them, and how it affects you?

Some time ago, a great swami was invited to stay with our family for five days. As Swamiji came to the dinner table, my mother served five dishes that she had cooked in his honor. When Swamiji saw those five dishes, he made the comment that "You have cooked food for five days, because I need and take only one dish with each meal."

My mother said, "Swamiji, today you take all five dishes, however, tomorrow I shall make only one."

Swamiji said, "When I can fulfill my need with one dish, why do I need five? The food that you have made today is good for five days." He continued, "You have invited me to stay with you for five days so that I could impart some spiritual knowledge to you. Since you have already done the cooking for the remainder of the four days, now you can spend more of your time conversing with me on spiritual topics such as yoga, meditation, and prayer. That would be good for you as well as me."

Swamiji stressed that happiness is the product of contentment, which comes when one focuses on needs, and not wants. Needs are limited and easy to fulfill. However, wants can be limitless and hard to fulfill and therefore, can be a cause of misery and unhappiness. (This point of difference between needs and wants has been also discussed by his Holiness the Dalai Lama, in his book *The Art of Happiness*.)

Secret # 41. Why did Mahatma Buddha (the prince) abandon the luxury of the palace to became a monk?

Mahatma Buddha was the founder of the Buddhist religion and was one of the greatest souls in human history. You might know that he was a prince as a little boy.

What brought the change in his life? Firstly, he was sensitive and a kind child to begin with. But three incidents occurred that made him question, what is life? The first was sickness, the second old age and the third the sight of a dead body. Thereafter, he decided that he must find out how one can liberate oneself from the cycle of birth and death. To fulfill his search, he left the palace and became a monk. He meditated constantly for 12 years till he achieved enlightenment.

Finally, he came to the realization that the real source of happiness is the inner self and not the external world. He further concluded that to get in touch with the inner self, one must meditate regularly. That is an important path to happiness.

The contributions of Mahatma Buddha are tremendous, and he will be remembered for many generations to come. He has shown how anyone can have access to happiness, by the simple technique of meditation, the technique of connecting with the inner self.

For clarification's sake, there are two paths to life, materialism and spiritualism. We all know that there is a constant struggle inside the heart and mind of many over which path to choose. While materialism provides comfort and luxuries, at times it can take one away from the path of happiness, whereas spiritualism offers happiness and bliss but often one may have to sacrifice the luxuries and comforts of life.

I believe there is a path between the two, which is not that hard, but one must want to do it. What is the secret? To my understanding the secret is to live the spiritual life, that is practice meditation and prayer, and exhibit altruism, but also enjoy the materialistic element without getting attached to material goods. This is also known as the principle of non-attachment. It may not be that easy to begin with, but at least one can aim for that. Of course, it requires practice and patience, but one day it does become second nature.

Secret #42. How to stop others from bothering you?

Once I was walking with a spiritual master and one of the people on the street started to make derogatory remarks about him. I looked at the master as if I was seeking his response, but the master started to laugh and said, "I am a fakir (swami/monk) and these words don't affect me."

The word fakir literally means a man with no ego. And as you know, the person who can get rid of his or her ego is not affected easily by the behavior of others.

This story has a second implied message, that it is the strength of the person—physical, mental or spiritual—that determines how easily a person can be affected by the circumstances, situations or even positive or negative comments of others.

So, stronger personalities are not affected easily by positive or negative situations, comments of others, whereas a person with weaknesses whether physical or mental, are affected easily by situations and circumstances as well as positive or negative comments of others. Some people say that

"Such and such person are too weak and you can make him/her dance to your tune."

In this reference let me quote from the Scriptures: "Water neither can dissolve a stone nor wet the lotus flower. It is because of the inherent and strong qualities of these two elements, that is why they are not affected by water."

People are people. Some people like to bother others for the reason unknown. But the best way to stop others from bothering you is to be strong physically and mentally. Then nobody will dare touch you.

Secret #43. Actions are wise, and reactions foolish.

Here is a little incident that has a powerful message. Once, Dr. Martin Luther King Jr. was walking down the street with a friend and when another person on the street started to make racist remarks, his friends looked at Dr. King and asked him, "Sir, people are making racist remarks at you! Do you wish to say something to them?"

Dr. King kept walking without paying attention to the remarks, and finally said, "I do not have to go to his level."

One's thoughtful actions are the reflection of one's wisdom. Whereas the quick reactions in response to the acts of others, without giving due thought can be foolish at times. Here the thinking process often takes a back seat.

Secret #44. How a wise man defeats hate with love? — A true story

There is a story about a great spiritual master, Maharishi Dayanand. Many times, he had to face many challenging and difficult situations. The fact was that Maharishi was a social reformer and one of his goals was to free the public from the trickery or the games of the leaders or pundits who took advantage of them. These leaders made several attempts to harm or even kill the master. However, the master challenged them successfully every time with his wisdom and/or physical strength.

Quite often, children were bribed by these leaders and pundits to throw stones at the Maharishi to hurt him. It is interesting to see how the master dealt with those situations. He kept calm and cool while dealing with children and never got angry. He knew that those children were innocent and it was the fault or the miss guidance of the religious leaders, or pundits and so on.

So, instead of getting angry, he offered children sweets and cookies to win their hearts. Finally, the children realized that this swami was of a higher caliber and did not deserve their mistreatment, and became friendly with him. Many times, these children revisited the spiritual master at his cottage for more sweets.

The great souls and the spiritual masters have unique ways of dealing with challenging situations. This is one incident where a master conquered hate with love. This spiritual master was unique and had more love for humanity than himself.

Secret #45. How high is the life of a person? — The measurement unit

It is strange but true that there are very few people who give real thought as to why they are born and/or what is the purpose of life. To the average person, life is a simple routine from birth until death. They are content if they can eat, get an education or college degree, get a job, have a family and become good providers.

I am going to share with you the story of a brave person who had a higher purpose in life, higher than his own life. This hero left a positive and great impact for many generations to come. This story will drop your jaw, leave your mouth open and will keep you wondering for a long time to come. This is the story of Mr. Bhagat Singh.

This story dates to before India gained independence. Mr. Bhagat Singh was a very young man. He was full of energy and enthusiasm. He gave his life for the freedom of India. His blood was boiling. He took every breath for the country and ate his food for the country. He was very distressed, restless and could not accept that mother India was ruled by the British government. To show his anger against the British government he threw a bomb at one of the government buildings. Thereafter he was arrested, prosecuted and sentenced to death.

The most intriguing and interesting part of the story was the dialogue that took place between Mr. Singh and the superintendent of the jail, the night before Mr. Singh was to be hanged to death.

To begin with, the superintendent asked him, "Mr. Singh, how do you feel?"

Mr. Singh started to laugh and said, "I could not be any better or happier than I am today." He continued, "I have taken this birth solely for this day and therefore my purpose is fulfilled."

The superintendent was taken a little back. He asked, "Mr. Singh, do you have any wish?"

Mr. Singh replied, "Yes — I wish I would come back in the next life right here in this jail to be hanged a second or even third time if I must, for the freedom of my country."

Finally, the superintendent asked him, "Are you not afraid of death?"

At this point, Mr. Singh opened the book that he used to read every day, the Bhagavad-Gita (one of the Scriptures of India), and read the following quote:

"The soul is eternal. Neither it takes birth, nor it dies. We the human beings are souls. The body is given to us as a vehicle for the soul to carry our duties. At the time of death, it is the body that dies and not the soul. The soul continues its journey to the next or new body. This process continues for eternity." Mr. Singh finally concluded, "Then what I should be afraid of?"

When the purpose of life is higher than the self, nothing can come in the way of a person's mission, and even death cannot scare him/her. The wise people say, "the higher the purpose, the higher the life."

Secret #46. Simple living and high thinking! — A spiritual model

Once I stayed at a convent for one week. This incident dates back to 10 years past. It was a homeopathic conference, and I had to stay at a convent because such was the arrangement of the managing committee. Many conferences are held at resorts, vacation places, convents and so on. However, this one was arranged at a convent.

During the week, besides learning from the conference, I had the opportunity to witness the life of the monks and the priests. Although all their basic needs were met, their life was limited as far as luxuries and comfort of life were concerned. What impressed me most was how these monks and priests lived so happily, because they all had a purpose to which they had devoted their entire lives.

At times, I hear negative comments from some people who say that the monks and priests have resigned from life. I tend to disagree with them. I believe monks and priests have a mission. They are the models of spirituality and we need all kinds of people on this earth to create a perfect balance. Without spirituality, materialism would rule and it could be disastrous.

The spiritual life has its own rewards, where the comforts and luxuries of life may have no meaning. It may be hard for some people to understand, but ask the spiritual ones, they know it all.

We do need to learn from them at least how to be at peace within ourselves

Secret #47. A brief interview with a Lama on the subject of life.

Once I was at the airport, and somehow my flight got delayed by two hours. I was sitting in the area where you must wait before you board the plane. It so happened that a respected lama was sitting there because he had to catch the same flight. I took an opportunity to introduce myself and started conversing with him with the intent to understand the life of a lama.

Lamas are a kind of monk. They come from the Himalayas in Nepal, north of India. His Highness the Dalai Lama is the head of all lamas.

I had a long discussion with him. However, here I would only share with you the important and pertinent part that will reflect some light on the life and the views of the lamas.

I asked Mr. Lama, "Are you sincerely happy with your life that you are living?" I asked this question because I was never sure why some people would choose this life.

He replied, "Yes, I am very happy. This is my choice. If I would have been married, maybe I would have three or four children and could help them. However, though I am single, I have a huge family of contacts, disciples, and teachers. I can serve them all. Not only this — now I have more opportunities to rise and prosper as well as help humanity."

Secret #48. The fastest way to learn happiness is to teach happiness.

Teaching is one of the best ways of learning or mastering a subject. Let me give you a good example. In my medical college days, I had a very clever professor who had a great teaching technique. Whenever he felt that a student had some weakness in any subject, he would ask the student to give a presentation on that topic to the class in the next few days. Therefore, the student was forced to study and master the subject for the presentation. This was how the professor made the student learn what they were deficient in.

To whom you should teach: Firstly, you should start with yourself, then your children and family, and thereafter anyone you can. Remember, when you teach your children, they will teach their children and so on. Thereby you are creating a generation of happy people, making a big contribution to the family and to the world.

Secret #49. The power of the commitment to a healthy and happy life.

In our society, when you ask a person how they feel, most will say reflexively, without thinking, "I feel fine." They may be miserable or even dying, but typically this is how people reply instantly. Why? It is a reflex response, and not one rooted in thought. The same is true in my clinic. However, most people correct the statement immediately by saying, "I am not fine, otherwise I would not be here."

However, I have a patient who is always happy. He is kind of a spiritual person, and whenever he comes to my office and I ask him how he feels, his typical response has been: "I feel fit and fine," and at other times, he will say, "I feel blessed." He further states, "If I don't feel this good now than when? I am responsible for my health and wellbeing; therefore, I take good care of myself."

The point I wish to stress is that this patient's response is a thoughtful, and not a reflex response, unlike the previous one. It is because of the fact that he has made a commitment for his health and well-being that is paying off. His statement makes me smile every time I see him.

Commitment is a very powerful tool. Once you make a commitment you can achieve anything.

Let me take you one step further: if you wish to know what is meant by good health? Health does not mean just to be healthy physically. One must be healthy at all levels, that is physical, mental, emotional and spiritual. At a physical level, one should be of the right weight, not obese or underweight. Exercising regularly, consuming plenty of fruits and vegetables. At the mental level, one should have good and positive thoughts and make no room for negativity, at least not for long. Finally, spiritually speaking one should be happy, because without happiness there is no perfect health.

Spirituality:

Next, I shall discuss why spirituality is so important and what its secrets are?

Why spirituality? Spirituality means that which relates to the spirit or the soul. You need to know that we are in the spirit, and the spirit is the essence of life. Spirituality is one of the ways to happiness.

Human life has three components, the body, mind and soul/spirit. And it is the spirit that tops the hierarchy of the system. Spirituality helps the person to connect with his or her inner self, the source of all happiness. Almost all spiritual people are happy. At least, this has been my observation.

What are the spiritual lessons/techniques? The techniques that help the person to connect with his or her inner self. This can include meditation, observation of silence, prayer, internal cleansing such as fasting, speaking the truth, staying fit physically and mentally, yoga, and so on.

Let us look at the definition of the word "spirituality." The Oxford English Dictionary defines spirituality as relating to or affecting the human spirit, as opposed to the material or physical body. The second definition given by the dictionary is, spirit means courage and/or energy.

Let me clarify further by giving an opposing example. When one says that a person has no spirit, it means he or she has no energy or courage. He/she is just a living body.

Secret #50. Meditation — an easy path to happiness!

Meditation is probably the most commonly practiced technique to connect with the inner self and hence find happiness. It has been my observation that people who meditate regularly are generally happy and successful, compared to those who do not meditate. Of course, there are many happy and successful people who do not meditate.

Meditation has multiple advantages. One of the most important ones is, it increases the level of consciousness and the level of alertness, a unique combination. In addition, it calms down the wandering and restless mind, an important cause of many miseries. It prolongs life and makes one more productive. And finally, it helps to connect with the inner self, the source of all peace and happiness.

As far as history is concerned, meditation came from India. The father of yoga was Maharishi Patanjali, one of the greatest saints of India.

The discipline of yoga has eight steps and meditation is one of them. There are several meditation techniques. However, I can say from my experience that they all work. The real key to the success of meditation is not the technique one chooses but how sincere, committed and/or regular a person is in his or her practice.

If you ask me is there an easy technique to meditation, I would say, yes. Although there are several techniques, as I have mentioned above, the simplest is to recite a word or phrase, a "mantra," over and over in quite rapid succession. That helps your mind not to wander and to get focused. Thus, the mind and the person both get relaxed and energized. What word or mantra one uses will depend on the person's choice. However, I can say that the most common word or sound that is used often, is AUM ("om").

Another commonly asked question is how often one needs to meditate and for how long. It is recommended that meditation should be practiced twice a day for a minimum of 20 minutes each. However, the longer the better.

You also need to know that the benefits of meditation are cumulative. So more you do it, the more you will gain from it.

Many people get discouraged in the early part of the practice of meditation. They often comment that their mind still wanders and they are ready to give up. I have been responding to them emphatically, please do not give up or worry, just keep practicing. Every time you practice meditation your mind will wander less and less. However, you may or may not be able to appreciate that in the beginning. I know from my own experience that I have been meditating more than 50 years, yet at times my mind still wanders. It does not mean I'm not getting the benefits. I can say emphatically that meditation has saved my life.

The second and next most common comment people make is that 20 minutes a day is quite a wastage of time. My response is that the practice of meditation makes one far more productive in life. That alone can save a tremendous amount of time, several folds more than the time spent in meditation. This is in addition to the many other benefits mentioned above.

I have been also observing that every year, more and more people are turning to the practice of meditation than ever before. It is also important to know that meditation is an aspect of spirituality and has no religious association, and therefore is for everyone.

If you are not a meditator at this time, it may be the proper time to start. There is a tremendous amount of information available about meditation everywhere.

Secret #51. Silence: the time for inner reflection, self-growth and happiness!

All man's miseries derive from not being able to sit quietly in his room alone.
— *Blaise Pascal*

The Oxford English Dictionary defines silence as a complete absence of sound, or the act or state of abstaining from speech or avoidance of mentioning or discussing.

During a period of silence, the person stays calm and composed. During this period, one focuses on his or her weaknesses or shortcomings, with the intention to remove them. You may call it inner reflection. During this period, one also tries not to interact with others by means of speech, writing or gestures. The duration of the period of silence can vary from hours to days. (In rare cases, among spiritual masters, even months.)

During this period, a person usually stays alone, or in the company of his or her religious books or literature. However, one can do his or her work, if one so chooses.

Let me narrate one interesting incident from my childhood in this reference. I was about ten years old when my father decided to visit a swami in his ashram, in the city of Jagadhari, in the state of UP, India.

This swami was well known as a yogi — his name was Swami Atma Nand. We took a train from our hometown to the city where the swami had his ashram. After getting off the train we walked approximately a mile to get to his ashram. When we arrived, the Swamiji was sitting under a tree with 20 other saints in a circle and of course, Swamiji in the center. We bowed our heads and sat down. After one hour or so, we left. During this one-hour period nobody uttered a word, neither us, nor Swamiji or anybody else. Not even a greeting of any kind. I did not think much of that at that time, but now I often think of that experience and appreciate it.

It is a great tool for people who are concerned with every minute of their time. Silence is one of the easiest techniques for self- growth and development and therefore happiness. The other benefits includes that one learns to restrain and control oneself. It is also one of the best ways to practice spirituality.

Silence is different from meditation. During meditation, one tries to focus on one word or sound, so that you can stop your mind from going in a thousand directions, whereas during the practice of silence one find time for inner reflection. Both practices of silence and meditation are examples of spirituality, and they are complementary to each other.

Secret #52. The prayer — one of the best ways to charge one's life batteries

Many spiritual masters have stated that the longer you sit with Him, the stronger your life batteries will be. Since prayer carries different meanings to different people, let me begin this lesson with a definition. The simplest definition of the word prayer is "solemn requests for help or expressions of thanks addressed to God or another deity." However, if you wish to define the word prayer little more deeply, in that case, we need to go Vedic scriptures. Per them, prayer has three components:

The first component is sitting with God. Being in the company of the supreme, who is perfect, blissful and Almighty. What a special opportunity, to sit with the supreme!

The second component is reciting the qualities of God. As you know, the qualities or attributes of God are numerous, as He is the model of perfection. Vedas have given more than 100 qualities or attributes to God. One may recite as many attributes or qualities as one wishes. The more the better.

Many people ask, what is the purpose of reciting the attributes of God? In response, Scripture has stated that when you recite something over and over, eventually that begins to trickle or rub into your life.

The third and last component of prayer is asking for something. Unfortunately, for many, this is the real meaning of prayer. Per Scripture, prayer must be selfless.

You all have heard thousands of times that a person is known by the company they keep. In other words, if you live with the lame you also become lame, but if you live with the people of courage and power you also become courageous and strong. Simple enough, but powerful.

Next, think that during the prayer you're spending your time with the supreme, Almighty and source of all good and energy. Can you imagine how it can affect your life?

Prayer is one of the greatest ways to charge your life batteries so that you can feel better and stronger and lead a happier life. You cannot appreciate the benefits without practicing.

Many people think that meditation and prayer are the same. Prayer and meditation may look similar, but they are different. During prayer, you talk to God or sit with him, whereas during meditation one tries to achieve a state of relaxation by controlling one's restless mind.

One of my friends has a unique way of differentiating the two, he states that in prayer you talk to God, whereas in meditation God talks to you. This is his way. I do not know how true that is, but I have inserted these lines for your consideration.

Secret #53. The curse of the golden pen.

I mentioned earlier that my father used to take all of us to the spiritual master's periodically so that we could learn something about spirituality. Since I have attended many discourses from different swamis, here is one of them about non-attachment.

"Non-attachment is the way to freedom and happiness," said the master. He further added that it is important to understand that attachment and non-attachment are opposites. He continued, saying that attachment is one of the root causes of human suffering. The more attached you get to anything, the more freedom you lose and the more likely you are to suffer, and conversely the more detached you stay in life, the more freedom and liberty you will enjoy, and the less likely you are to suffer. He further stressed the point that attachment is a shackle of the human being.

You need to remember that attachment can be to anything, it can be to family, a person, or any personal belongings such as a house, clothes, even a pen.

Swamiji gave the following example. "During my school days, there was a boy in class who was from a very average family. However, one of his relatives was very rich. On one of his birthdays, his rich relative gave him a golden pen. Before the student got this golden pen, he was a happy boy and very kind natured. He was also very good in his studies. He used to help other students out of good will and was of a very giving nature. However, after getting this golden pen, he became a different person. He used to worry a lot about his golden pen and lost his pleasant demeanor. Now, if anybody would ask for his pen, he would get angry. He lost many friends because of his new behavior. Also, his grade in the class started to fall. Unfortunately, one day, he lost his golden pen and that became a day of misery for him. He became depressed, all due to his attachment to the golden pen."

All human beings are born free and happy, and you can perceive that in almost all children. It is because they are neither attached nor worry about anything. They leave all their worries to their parents. Unfortunately, when people become adults, they start to get more and more attached and worry and therefore start to lose their happiness. Finally, a time comes when attachment takes over the person's life and he/she become the slave of the things that he/she possesses. This is called attachment.

Attachment and non-attachment are two sides of a coin. Where the attachment is the cause of pain and misery, non-attachment is a path to happiness.

Secret #54. The power of the mighty truth!

Truth is so powerful that some people say, the truth is God and God is a truth.

Swami Vivekananda in his writing has stated, a person who can speak the truth for twelve consecutive years can become godly. It is a powerful statement coming from a such a great swami.

I have met all kinds of people. There are some people who usually speak the truth, and then there are others who barely tell the truth, to whom lying is a routine. Or you can say that they lie even without realizing that they are lying. Of course, most people are in between.

I have also come to appreciate the fact that people who speak the truth are sincere to themselves and others and have no fears and are generally happy. Whereas people who lie by habit are usually nervous and insecure in themselves, and therefore lose their happiness.

There is one more fact in reference to the truth; that is that the truth should not be bitter. For example, calling a thief a thief, or calling a liar a liar is a bitter truth, and is not good for anyone including the person who makes such a statement. Therefore, it has no place in daily life.

If you wish to study this idea further, I can refer you to a classic story of an Indian king, Harish Chandra, who never lied in his life and could even win the heart of God.

Speaking the truth is another powerful secret for happiness.

Secret # 55. Should you forgive?

Forgiveness has many rewards in itself. However, it is easier said than done. The question remains, should you forgive or not?

It is very hard to answer this question. It is a judgment call of the person who had to make such a decision. Each person is different and there are many factors involved in making such a decision. However, the following article may be of help.

The Oxford English Dictionary has defined forgiveness as to stop being angry or resentful for an offense or a mistake.

When does the question of forgiveness come? It has been the observation of many that whenever there are fights, quarrels, or strong disagreement, it often creates a vicious cycle. And that cycle needs to be broken, otherwise the situation continues to get worse. There are two ways to do it: first the compromise, and second the forgiveness. You know that many times in life, compromise is not a possibility. It could be that the other person is ignorant or may have an ego problem. In those cases, forgiveness is the only answer.

Let me offer two examples to clarify my point.

I have a female patient in her early sixties who came to me very distressed and complaining of a headache. She has told me she never had a headache in her life because she is a very relaxed person. She's very religious and goes to church every Sunday along with her husband. At this visit, she did not tell the whole story. I counseled her and prescribed some medication.

I saw her again after six weeks. Now, she disclosed the whole facts. She told me that her husband had been cheating on her. She further told me that now the family was going to marriage counseling and it was helping her. Now, she looked relaxed and had no more headaches. She also told me that her husband had apologized deeply and she had forgiven him. She further stated that ever since she had forgiven him, she felt much better; before this she used to be angry all the time and it was affecting not only her but also the whole family. She further told me that her religion teaches forgiveness.

Next, let me share a classical story of Lord Buddha.

At the beginning of the foundation of the Buddhist religion, the Lord was not loved by many; as a matter of fact, many people hated him. Some hated him so much that they would not let him stay in their villages as he was traveling. Therefore, he had to go through tough times. You might know that Lord Buddha traveled from one village to another on foot for the purpose of spreading his philosophy.

One day while visiting a village, a person came to see him. He was an angry man. He cursed and spoke words of hate to the Lord and finally spit in his face. Lord Buddha kept calm and asked him, "Do you have anything else to say?" The man yelled again and left still angry.

As time passed, the angry man realized that his actions were unjust and unfair. He started to repent and to feel more guilty. He started to hate himself for his actions. The time came that his own action became a cause of misery for him. He began to lose sleep. Finally, he came to the realization that he must apologize to the Lord, to find peace within himself. However, it was not easy to find the master because he had no address. He was just a traveler.

Two years later, Lord Buddha happened to visit the same village once again. The man came to see the Lord, touched his feet and asked for forgiveness for his prior act. The Lord replied, in a gentle tone, "My dear child, I have forgiven you on the very first day, because I could not find a place for the anger in my heart." Thereafter, this man became a disciple of the Mahatma.

Such is the power of forgiveness. Can you imagine how much suffering this angry man went through for two years after the episode of his own anger? Also appreciate how the great master never suffered, because he forgave the person on day one.

Wise people say forgiveness is one of the best ways to unload one's own pain and find ease within oneself.

Secret #56. Put a smile on their faces and they will put one on yours!

This chapter is a little heavier in the sense that you need to pay a little more attention than other chapters. It is intended for those who are little more mature than average, are independent and are searching for a deeper level of happiness and satisfaction in their lives.

Only a couple of days ago, I met a female patient in my clinic for the first time. She is a very happy and charming person. She is in her seventies but I would not have guessed her to be more than sixty.

She told me that she has four children. Two of them are her own and two of them are adopted. She further told me that her own children are in their late forties and are doing extremely well. One is an engineer and the other is a doctor. Her two adopted children are handicapped.

I asked her, "You adopted two handicapped children?"

She told me that she used to work for Dreyfus, an organization that helps children who are neglected or not cared for properly. She explained that she was a nurse for Dreyfus. She realized that these two children were not properly cared for, so she adopted them.

She further stated that she was doing her best in taking care of those two children. She felt she had contributed greatly to their lives. She was a proud and happy woman. This is an example of extreme giving.

You know, giving and receiving are two aspects of life. And there are two corresponding phrases in the literature. Let us analyze them here.

Phrase #1: God helps those who help themselves.

Phrase #2: God helps those who help others.

Next, think for a minute; which one is correct?

You have probably guessed right. Both are correct. It depends upon the phase of life. For simplicity's sake, life can be divided into two phases:

1. Early phase: growth and development.

2. Later phase: independence, maturity and wisdom.

Let us begin with the early phase of growth and development. This stage begins from the time of birth till you become independent. That includes infancy, childhood, schooling, graduate or postgraduate education and even vocational training, till you to become independent in life.

This is the receiving phase of life. You cannot grow up without receiving. It is perfectly okay to receive in this stage. You receive support from your parents in every possible manner whether financial, physical, mental, emotional, intellectual, or spiritual. Without them you cannot exist in this world.

Later on, you receive support from teachers, coaches, uncles and aunts, good friends and so on. If you are lucky enough you might receive support even from a stranger. But the point is that every well-wisher keeps telling you the same thing, grow up. They all tell you, "God helps those who help themselves." They all try to convey the message that if you don't help yourself, nobody can help you.

The first phrase is perfectly applicable to this stage of growth and development. Of course, receiving is okay while one is in the phase of growth and development or dependency and helplessness.

Next you arrive at the second phase of life, where you are independent, mature and hopefully wiser. Here is a big shift in your life. Up till now you were in receiving mode, however now you are in a giving mode. If you are married you will support your family, your spouse and so on. Not only this; you become an asset to the place where you work, your community, and the organizations to which you belong. Now, you begin to take pride in yourself. People look up to you with respect. Because now you're doing something for others.

Now you also begin to reflect on your earlier life. How your parents have made sacrifices to bring you up to that stage. You also begin to realize the support that you have received from your teachers, coaches and mentors and even strangers. Most importantly, you begin to realize that life is not all about receiving, but giving.

You begin to realize that when you do something for others rather than for yourself, it gives you a greater pleasure and happiness. This is the stage where the second phrase I mentioned earlier is applicable: "God helps those who help others."

There is also a corresponding phrase in India which is as follows:

Kar Bhala,

Ho Bhala,

Antt Me,

Bhale Ka Bhala.

It means, when you do good to others it comes back to you in a positive manner. As a result, everybody benefits.

So, a mature and wise person realizes that life is not all about receiving, but rather giving. Of course, it is true that you can give only if you have it. In other words, you can give only of the area in which you are stronger whether it is physical, emotional, intellectual spiritual or financial and so on.

The universal fact remains, "Giving is greater than receiving." Making somebody happy will add to your happiness and a much deeper satisfaction.

Secret #57. Yoga: an introduction

You may ask why I am discussing yoga in this book? There are several reasons for that such as: 1.Yoga is the science of physical and mental well-being and everlasting happiness.

2. The knowledge of yoga is very sacred. It was kept as a secret for thousands of years from the common people until recently when a spiritual master took a bold step to make sure that everybody has an access to this valuable gift. Strange it may be, women were never allowed to have this knowledge. It was offered only to the men that also of the people with the highest caliber such as Kings, yogis, spiritual masters and so on. Therefore, I believe that the most people are not aware how valuable this information is.

3. I thought I should give a good glimpse about yoga at least in brevity, so that it may spark some interest in the reader who wants to take their happiness at the highest level.

4. Finally, Yoga is very much misunderstood in the Western world.

Although, Yoga is an art and science of total well-being of the person at physical, mental and spiritual levels, and has eight stages of development. However, many Westerners think that yoga is just a practice of postures and meditation. At the most, some are happy to include breath control. This is not complete yoga and hence does not give you all the benefits of yoga.

Let me make an important comment before going any further. If you ask me can you create heaven on this earth, I would say yes. This is how? You all know that you perceive the world from our own perspective. For example, happy people feel that everyone is happy, and sad people believe that the world is miserable. Therefore, when one attains blissfulness in his or her life, he/she also begins to see the bliss all around him or her. This gives one a heavenly feeling.

The praise of yoga: the science of yoga has glorious praises all over the literature including the Scriptures itself. Following are some examples:

This is what Veda [the book of knowledge] states:

Nothing exceeds the excellence of man who is the combination of the body, mind, intellect, and the atma (soul).

Na hi manushat shreshthataram hi kinchit maha bharat.

Vedas

The Upanishad explains yoga as follows: Yoga means union with the self or the supreme. Union with self means that the physical, mental, and spiritual components of the individual are in harmony with each other. This happens only when one is balanced and healthy at all three levels; then one is in touch with the inner self. It is then only that one becomes content, peaceful, and attains bliss.

The Bhagavad-Gita glorifies yoga as follows: "The tongue cannot describe the happiness that communion with the self (or God) brings, when the ignorance and other like impurities have been washed away by the needs of yogic samadhi, and the self- rising within itself concentrates on God."

Its further states, when you meet a person whose face is lustrous, who is happy and joyous, who is calm, content and at peace within himself, and emanates peace to others, you can consider that person a yogi.

While we are on the subject of praise of yoga, let me say a few words of mine. Most people are not aware how lucky they are to be able to have access to knowledge about yoga. In ancient times the knowledge of yoga was kept secret and was imparted only to people of the highest caliber such as kings, princes, Rishis and high-ranking priests and so on. Does not it shock or surprise you that such a useful science was kept secret from the common people?

However, a couple of hundred years ago a few Rishis took a bold step to bring this information to the public. And one of the well-known persons responsible for bringing this information to the public was a great saint known as, Maharishi Dayanand Sarasvati.

Definition of yoga:

The word "yoga" is derived from the Sanskrit word *yuj* meaning to join or come together. The English word "yoke" has the Sanskrit root. A yoke is a wooden stick which joins two oxen together while working in the field. Literally speaking, yoga is used when two things join together. Similarly, when all three levels of human being – physical, mental, and spiritual – are in harmony with each other, a person becomes complete and whole. This is yoga.

According to the Oxford English Dictionary, yoga is a Hindu spiritual and ascetic discipline, a part of which includes breath control, simple meditation, and adoption of specific bodily postures.

Patanjalli states: "Yoga is the complete and ultimate control of all mental activities," or *yoga-schitta-vrtti-nirodhah*.

Lord Krishna in *Gita* states: "Yoga is maintenance of emotional equilibrium in adversities, as well as in favorable circumstances (*samatvam yoga Uchyate*)."

Behold the statement of Swami Vivekananda, how he describes in depth the characteristics of a yogi: "The one who finds in the middle of intense activity the greatest rest, and in the middle of greatest rest intense action is a yogi. Yogi can attain that highest state of mind, which is super concentration."

The cause of human suffering per scriptures:

You may ask why human beings suffer, and how yoga can help? According to *Upanishad*, human beings are divine because they come from the divine. Therefore, there is no place for suffering. The suffering happens only when human being loses their self-identity. To give you an example, when human beings become bonded or attached to the temporary and mundane issues of life, they also become temporary and mundane, and that is the cause of suffering. However, the science of yoga makes you realize that you are eternal and the source of all bliss and joy. That is your innate nature. This realization brings joy and bliss.

Have you ever wondered about the state of mind of a suffering person? According to *Upanishad*, the state of mind of suffering human beings can be compared with the state of mind of the "lost child."

Here, let me know narrate the story of the lost child from the literature. A child goes with his mother to a busy fair. The child asks his mother for a balloon, but his mother refuses to buy one. As they walk a few steps further, the child asks for a candy but the mother again refuses to buy any. The mother keeps on walking. Then the child asks his mother if he can go on a ride, but his mother also refuses that. All of a sudden, the child is detached from his mother and gets lost and starts crying. As you know, the fair is a busy place and crowded with people. Everybody's busy having fun and running in a hundred directions. Not an easy place to find anyone, especially children.

Thereafter, his mother goes crazy in search of her son. However, some good Samaritans find the lost child. They take pity and try to comfort and console the child, but he does not stop crying. People offer him balloon, candy, rides, but he refuses everything and does not want anything. He continues to cry and states, "I want only my mother." I want only my mother and nothing else. Suddenly his mother finds him. Now he starts laughing. He clings to his mother. She also holds him very tightly for her own relief. Now the child gets a balloon, and he is very happy with it.

That is state of the suffering person. When he/she loses one's identity, and forgets his or her eternal and joyous nature, he/she suffers and becomes restless and cannot find peace or happiness anywhere. Yoga helps people to realize once again the real nature of being and they attain bliss again.

Next, I want to bring a very important point to your attention: that every species produces its own kind. The orange tree produces oranges. The mango tree produces mangoes, and the coconut tree produces coconuts, and so on. Since we are the children of divine God, we must be divine by nature. Therefore, suffering has no place in life. If we suffer it is our own fault.

Branches of yoga:

Yoga is a contribution of the seers or spiritual masters of India. The spiritual master who made it a philosophy and a science with clear direction is known by the name of Patanjali Rishi. He lived 200 B.C. All branches of yoga follow Patanjali yoga.

There are four branches of yoga and all have the same common goal. One can choose any one of these or any combination of them.

Dhyana or Raja Yoga (yoga of meditation)

This is essentially meditation. The mind is restless, fleeting, and wandering in nature. When we meditate, our mind becomes focused on one point, and we begin to appreciate real joy, peace, and contentment within ourselves.

Karma Yoga (yoga of action)

When a man helps others without seeking any reward for himself, he is said to be karma yogi. He becomes like the Lord and starts to perceive Him within himself. This is exactly what God does. It is popular with people who love to help their fellow beings.

Janani Yoga (Yoga of knowledge)

In this branch of yoga, a man seeks truth by means of intelligence and logic. This is in favor with people who are philosophers or who tend to think in a logical manner.

Bhakti Yoga (yoga of devotion)

Here the devotee surrenders himself totally at the feet of the Lord. He loves God as his mother. Mother is the most revered word in the dictionary. This branch is a favorite with people who are very simpleminded, emotional, and devoted to God. Here one gets rid of the ego and totally merges with God.

There are other branches of yoga such as kundalini yoga, Hatha yoga, laughing yoga, etc., that I am not going to discuss here, because this is not a book on yoga.

The Eight stages of yoga:

The science of yoga, as laid out by the Patanjali Rishi, consists of eight stages. Therefore, it is known as Astanga Yoga (*asta* means eight, *anga* means steps). These are as follows:

1. Yama, (moral conduct), five in number
2. Niyama, (physical and religious observance), five in number
3. Asana, correct postures to still bodily restlessness
4. Prana Yama, control of *prana*, subtle life currents and mind
5. Pratyahara, interiorization
6. Dharna, concentration
7. Dhyana, meditation

8. Samadhi, the ecstasy of oneness with God/or with self

Here is a brief discussion about the eight stages of yoga:

Stage 1: Yama or restraint (moral conduct, principle of self-control) – Five Commandments

Non-violence

This is the principle of co-existence with all. To love every human being and not to think, say, or do bad. The biggest advantage of this principle is that the sense of enmity (malice) towards all creatures disappears from the mind. Jealousy is considered a violent act, according to Vedas.

Truth

To speak the truth about whatever is seen, listened to, read, and inferred in the mind. The advantage of this is that when people speak the truth, they become respectable and trustworthy with every being that they meet.

Abstention from theft

Not to take anything from anybody without permission, in thought, speech, or action. By such a practice a person achieves spiritual qualities. Vedas says if the thought of stealing comes to one's mind, even if one does not steal, one is a thief in a real sense, although one may not be a thief in the public's view.

Celibacy

To protect physical powers, one should not waste semen. The advantage of celibacy is that one's mind, speech, body, and intellect become strong. This is based upon the writing of the Scriptures, Vedas and Taoism. However, the modern generation does not believe in this.

Renunciation

No hoarding, no storing harmful and unessential objects or thoughts. The advantage is that one rises to a spiritual level, and realizes who they are.

Stage 2: Niyama or self-discipline: five commandments

Purification of body and the mind

Purification of the body is easy: keeping it clean, bathing, and eating healthy food. Purification of the mind means to tell the truth, study religious books, practice religious conduct, and so on. The advantage of this stage is that the mind remains concentrated and cheerful.

Satisfaction

To be satisfied with whatever is gained in the form of pleasure, teaching, power, wealth, and so on. The advantage being that one is happy, content, and at peace with the self.

Penance (Tap)

Not to get upset with hunger, cold, heat, loss, gain, and other dualities of life. The advantage being that one becomes strong and in charge of one's own mind.

Self-study, reading of the Vedas or other scriptures

Study and knowledge are essential for mental and spiritual growth and development.

Ishwar-Pranidhan (surrender to God)

To accept God's gift and surrender to God completely.

Stage 3: Asana (yoga postures)

The mind and body are deeply and directly connected with each other. Not only does the mind have an effect on the body, but the body also has an effect on the mind. You may have noticed that children who suffer from hyperactivity not only have a restless mind, but also a fidgety body. By the practice of Asana, the body and mind start working in coordination with each other. The body and mind calm down; such is the value of Asana.

Stage 4: Pranayama

Pranayama is disciplining Prana, the subtle energy which pervades and controls all of the functions of the body. Pranayama is a special method of breath control with which the life force is brought under control. This is achieved by controlling the incoming or outgoing breaths. The results can be further intensified by reciting the word OM while doing the Pranayama. Further, Pranayama helps to bring involuntary actions such as respiration and heartbeat under voluntary control. It takes practice to achieve the desired results. How does one control prana? It is a technique of deep and slow breathing, while keeping the mind focused on the breath. To understand more clearly, let us study the act of breathing.

The act of breathing: four components

The first component consists of the act of inhaling (breathing in), which should be very deep and very slow. The second component consists of holding the breath in as long as one can comfortably do. The third component consists of exhaling very slowly. The fourth component consists of holding the breath out as long as possible without any discomfort.

In a nutshell, each act of inhaling and exhaling should be a slow and deep process. Each act of breathing out should take twice the time than that of breathing in. For example, if you take ten seconds to inhale, then you should take twenty seconds to exhale. Or if you take five seconds to inhale, then you should take ten seconds to exhale and so on. Further you need to focus so that each act of breathing in is energizing to the body and the mind, and each act of breathing out is relaxing to the body.

There are different names given to the different acts of breathing in or breathing out, as follows:

Purak: This is the way of drawing in breath slowly and deeply to your full capacity.

Stambhak: This is retention of the breath (either holding it in or out).

Rechak: This is the way of letting your breath out slowly and to the maximum capacity.

Importance and advantages of Pranayama

1. The mind becomes stable.
2. You become more intelligent.
3. The pulse and heart rate slow down, so the heart has more time to relax and will have a longer life.
4. You need fewer breaths per minute. Number 3 and 4 cause prolongation of life.
5. Some yogis have mastered and controlled their breaths to the extent that they can hold their breath up to twenty-four hours or more, and can suspend their life force during that period.

Stage 5: Pratyahara (sense control)

In Pratyahara one withdraws attention from external sensory stimulus by redirecting it inwards. In the beginning, you develop discipline over your appetite by controlling your hunger, and you discipline the feeling of lust through divine support. Pratyahara also includes the appropriate nutritious intake of vegetarian food to achieve longevity and a healthy life by disciplining the mind over sensual desires. It is a stage of introspection, redirection, and arousal of inward energy. Pratyahara paves the way for improved focus and voluntary restraint of the emotions, the higher wakeful state of inner self, and the consciousness; this leads to satisfaction and contentment.

Stage 6: Dharana

Meditative concentration.

Stage 7: Dhyana

Intense meditation, complete submersion in meditation.

Stage 8: Samadhi

Transcendental absorption of consciousness with the absolute, infinite, divine super-consciousness, and to experience the bliss of the union.

A test of mental and spiritual growth and development

This test is based upon the ten commandments of yoga, or the first two stages of yoga: The Five Yamas and Five Niyamas. These commandments are responsible for the building of moral, ethical, and physical discipline. Therefore, they are the prerequisite for self-realization.

This test was originally devised by a great swami. He would not like to be credited, so his identity is not disclosed. Thanks to him

This test not only helps you to facilitate the understanding of the first two stages of yoga, but also gives you an opportunity to test yourself on a regular basis, as you travel on the path of yoga. This test is for your insight only. I suggest that the result should be kept confidential.

The Yamas – Restraints

AHIMSA – NONINJURY: I harm others by thoughts, words, or deeds.

1. Never 2. Rarely 3. Sometimes 4. Often

SATYA – TRUTHFULNESS: I refrain from lying and betraying promises.

1. Always 2. Usually 3. Sometimes 4. Rarely

ASTEYA – NONSTEALING: I steal, covet or enter into debt.

1. Never 2. Rarely 3. Sometimes 4. Often

BRAHMACHARIYA – SEXUAL PURITY: I control lust by remaining celibate when single or faithful in marriage.

1. Always 2. Usually 3. Sometimes 4. Rarely

KSHAMA – PATIENCE: I restrain intolerance with people and impatience with circumstances.

1. Always 2. Usually 3. Sometimes 4. Rarely

DHRITI – STEADFASTNESS: I overcome non-perseverance, fear, indecision and changeableness.

1. Always 2. Usually 3. Sometimes 4. Rarely

DAYA – COMPASSION: I conquer callous, cruel and insensitive feelings toward all beings.

1. Always 2. Usually 3. Sometimes 4. Rarely

ARJAVA – HONESTY: I renounce deception and wrongdoing.

1. Always 2. Usually 3. Sometimes 4. Rarely

MITAHARA – MODERATE APPETITE: I eat too much or consume meat, fish, fowl or eggs.

1. Never 2. Rarely 3. Sometimes 4. Often

SAUCHA – PURITY: I avoid impurity in body, mind and speech.

1. Always 2. Usually 3. Sometimes 4. Rarely

Your total score for the Yamas: _____

The Niyamas – Practices

SANTOSHA – CONTENTMENT: I seek joy and serenity in life.

1. Always 2. Usually 3. Sometimes 4. Rarely

TAPA – AUSTERITY: I perform sadhana, penance, tapas and sacrifice.

1. Regularly 2. Often 3. Sometimes 4. Rarely

DANA – CHARITY: I give charity without thought of reward.

1. Always 2. Usually 3. Sometimes 4. Rarely

ASTIKYA – FAITH: I believe firmly in GOD, Gods, guru and the path to enlightenment.

1. Always 2. Usually 3. Sometimes 4. Rarely

ISVARAPUJANA – WORSHIP: I cultivate devotion through daily worship and meditation.

1. Without fail 2. Often 3. Sometimes 4. Rarely

MATI – COGNITION: I develop spiritual will and intellect with a guru's guidance.

1. Always 2. Often 3. Sometimes 4. Rarely

SIDDHANTASRAVANA – SCRIPTURAL STUDY: I study the teachings and listen to the wise of my lineage.

1. Very often 2. Often 3. Sometimes 4. Rarely

HRI – REMORSE: I am modest and show shame for misdeeds.

1. Always 2. Usually 3. Sometimes 4. Rarely

VRATA – SACRED VOWS: I fulfill religious vows, rules, and observances faithfully.

1. Always 2. Usually 3. Sometimes 4. Rarely

JAPA – RECITATION: I chant holy mantras daily.

1. Always 2. Usually 3. Sometimes 4. Rarely

Your total score for the Niyamas: _____

Total score for both Yamas and the Niyamas: _____

The lower your score, the farther advanced you are on the spiritual path and less help you need to get on the right track. Take this test as often as you need to gauge your progress.

Here are your categories based on your combined scores:

20: Saintly person 50: Average struggler

25: Spiritually adept 55: Karma's slave

30: Advanced meditator 60: Bad example

35: Devout pathfinder 65: Selfish brute

40: Serious seeker 70: No one's friend

45: Good soul 75: Devious scoundrel

80: Dharma's (Religion's) enemy

Before concluding this chapter let me summarize once again the benefits of yoga for your memory, insight and consideration.

1. Your mind becomes clear and pure: This is the result of the first and second steps of Yama and Niyama.
2. Yoga improves coordination of the body and mind: the rewards of Asnas, the third stage of yoga.

3. Yoga helps to balance your mind: the first three stages of yoga plus Pranayama.

4. Yoga helps you feel contented and satisfied: the reward of the fifth step of yoga known as pratyahara.

5. Yoga helps to improve concentration till it becomes intense: the reward of the sixth and seventh stages of yoga.

6. Through yoga, you achieve union of the body, mind, and soul, the reward of the last stage of yoga known as Samadhi, i.e., union with self or the supreme. Now your consciousness expands, and you realize the real eternal nature of the self. You begin to enjoy the bliss of life.

Additional benefits

1. Your face becomes lustrous.
2. Your body becomes symmetrical.
3. You can control your heart rate and breathing.
4. Your intellect becomes sharp.
5. Your concentration becomes intense.
6. You begin to have true and beneficial thoughts.
7. Your consciousness expands; you feel content and blissful.

The regular practice of yoga creates harmonious relationship between your body, mind, and soul. When that happens, you realize that you are whole and complete. Thus, you do not need anything anymore. You have it all. You are an independent free human being on this huge planet.

This produces the deepest level of contentment, bliss and happiness. That is your ultimate goal.

I also have created the following mantra for you, that you can recite often. The more often the better.

"I will stay focused on the harmonious working of the body, mind, and soul to create a perfect balance for a better and happier life."

The Laughing Yoga

Since we are on the subject of yoga, let me briefly say something about laughing yoga.

Fake it, or make it.

It should be clear that simple laughing, or laughing yoga, is not the same as yoga in totality. Laughing is just a temporary act, whereas yoga provides eternal happiness. However, the fact remains that laughing is good for the body and mind. You all know the common proverb: "Happiness is the best medicine."

There's a lot of literature on laughing. Yoga has many branches and laughing yoga is just one of them. Yoga encourages people to laugh aloud till you cannot laugh anymore, or your belly starts to hurt and your eyes cannot stop watering. This is a great way to make oneself happy, at least temporarily.

Section 2

The Twelve Amazing Secrets from the Unhappy, Naïve and Miserable Ones

Let us switch gears. I sincerely hope that you must have enjoyed the first section of the book. It must have been rewarding experience to learn the 57 amazing secrets from wise and happy people. I believe it must have raised your happiness level at least to some degree. You also may be happy that you have finished the major section of the book. However, I want you to know that there's a lot more to come.

I will caution you that this upcoming section is quite different from the first one. In this section, you will be learning happy secrets indirectly, from the lives of unhappy, naïve and the miserable ones. If you ask me, can you learn from the unhappy and miserable people? I will answer yes; but you must use your analytical mind. This is how:

Firstly, you need to understand what elements or behaviors are responsible for the misery of these people and secondly, you need to learn how to avoid those. Simple enough!

Before going further, I want to caution you of the fact that the most negative elements or behaviors, such as fear, anxiety, greed, anger and so on, can be part of any human being's life at one time or another. It can be mine or even yours also. It is not abnormal, because no human being is perfect. However, the stories that I am presenting here are extreme examples, where the negative element, instead of being just a part of life, takes over a person's life. You can say that these people have become the victim of these elements. Therefore, I suggest that one should not be critical of them, rather one should have sympathy for them. Your focus should be to learn.

Since these are real life stories, I have changed the names to protect their identities. Now let us begin this interesting, analytical and intriguing study.

Secret #1. When "money focus" becomes a curse

Secret #2. How a "negative attitude" can make a person miserable

Secret #3. When one is too critical of others

Secret #4. Anxiety and worry — humans' worst enemies

Secret #5. Fear — the ghost

Secret #6. Can anger make a person a devil?

Secret # 7. How greed can destroy a family

Secret #8. The habit of "comparing" — the unfair and unethical game

Secret #9. Complaining — a nasty habit

Secret #10. When people let traffic (or anything) control their lives

Secret #11. How to deal with unpleasant, nasty and/or difficult people

Secret #12. Shoplifting — a never-ending curse

Secret #1. When "money focus" becomes a curse

The following story shows that when people's sole focus becomes money; they tend to forget or even ignore other valued aspects of life and thus become miserable. Such is the blinding glitter of money.

Tom came to me as a severely depressed patient. His wife was with him, and quite concerned. She stated that her husband could not sleep or eat, and did not even want to get out of bed. They had lost everything in their business. Here is the dialogue between Tom and me, in one of our clinical visits.

Dr.: How are you, Tom?

Tom: Yes, Doctor, my wife is right, I have lost everything. I have no energy, I'm depressed, and I hate to get out of bed.

Dr.: What do you mean by everything?

Tom: I mean everything. Once I used to have millions of dollars from my business, and now I don't have even 50% of that.

Dr.: So, you have lost close to 50%? How is your overall health? Do you have any other medical condition such as diabetes, blood pressure, or arthritis?

Tom: No, Doctor, I'm lucky in this regard, because I have no other medical condition. I have good genes. My both parents both lived into their eighties.

Dr.: Is your family okay?

Tom: Yes, I have two sons who work with me in the business. They are good boys and they are a big help, and they listen to me. They keep telling me, "Daddy, do not worry, we are okay."

Dr.: So, your family is with you and supportive of you?

Tom: Yes, my children and my wife are supportive of me, and without them, I would be dead today.

Dr.: How is your social life?

Tom: My social life is great. I'm a member of a church where I contribute a lot financially. Therefore, I enjoy good social status and have a lot of friends from the church, who often visit me and encourage me.

Dr.: Do you have enough money to eat and live on for some time to come?

Tom: Oh, this is not a problem. I have enough to live on for years and even my children do not have to worry about that, but the point is I have lost most of the money through my business.

Dr.: When did you start your business?

Tom: Seven years ago.

Dr.: How much did you invest in your business?

Tom: I had no money to start my business. I started from scratch, or maybe with very little investment. But I worked very hard to make the business flourish. I learned a lot from my father about business and my MBA degree has also helped me a lot.

Dr.: The way I understand it, your overall health is good, your family is together, your children and your wife are supportive of you, you have enough money to live on for many years, and you started your business with little or zero investment. As you have stated, you have lost only half of the money that you have earned from this business. You also know that money is not everything. Not only this, your children are telling you, daddy, we are still okay. The way I look at it is, you are not in bad shape. As a matter of fact, you should consider yourself lucky when you put all the facts together. Many people in your position would consider themselves lucky, and I certainly would.

Tom: Doctor, I think you do not understand me.

The wife started to laugh.'

I like to infer from the above story that when a person's sole focus becomes money; miseries are sure to follow. Tom's story is such an example. He has totally forgotten that his health and his family are still with him. He has lost sight of the fact that he started his business with zero investment. It is a sad story.

You know there are many similar stories of people with failed businesses. However, everybody does not get depressed. The depression or sadness takes over only when one loses the broader understanding of life and becomes too intensely focused on money, or as a matter of fact any single thing.

Secret #2. How a negative attitude can make a person miserable?

Attitude plays an extremely important role in life. It can make or break a person. As a positive attitude can be a cause of blessings, similarly a negative attitude can be the cause of curses.

One day while visiting Mrs. RM, I asked her how she was. This is the first question that I often ask to most of my patients when I meet them. It is like opening the conversation. But whenever I visited Mrs. RM, I always hesitated to ask this question, because I knew what what's coming next. However, neither she nor I could break our habits. So, I started my interview with Mrs. RM with the usual question, and she also replied with her three routine answers:

#1. "I feel terrible."

#2. "Nobody cares."

#3. "There is nothing good left in this world."

This has been her typical way of answering my question for years, as if a tape was playing inside her brain, although she was not depressed or sad by any medical standards.

One day, out of frustration, I asked one of her nephews, who was her guardian, about her demeanor and mentioned my concern about her statements. He told me, "Dr. Singhal, this is the way she is. She is not a happy person, and nobody can change her. She is financially strong but is very miserly. She has everything that she needs. Just do not pay attention to her words."

I was shocked to hear this from her nephew. Many times, Mrs. RM gave me the impression that she was very poor. At times, I even felt guilty charging her. She had been my patient for more than 10 years and I had seen her many times in my clinic as well as in the hospital, but she remained unchanged despite my repeated counseling.

Of course, it is true that habits and behaviors don't change easily and certainly not by themselves, unless one makes a sincere effort. You can also appreciate from this story that when a negative attitude takes over a person's life, all the goodness can disappear, and misery may be the only thing that remains.

Secret #3. When one is too critical of others?

People cannot hide anything from me or fool me, I know the devil in all of them
— Dr. Z

Here is the story of one of my colleagues. He not only had a negative view of everyone but was also critical of everyone, which made it doubly bad. He had the notion that people were bad and were hiding something from him. He always believed that he was the smartest person on earth. Whenever he would meet a person, even for the first time, he will start probing till he would find something wrong with them. If he could not, he would become uncomfortable or uneasy within himself and feel kind of defeated. His favorite statement was "I can judge a person from one mile away, people cannot fool me."

He himself was also not a pleasant person, and this was his typical demeanor. He got married and had one daughter. One day both his wife and daughter complained to me about his behavior. Therefore, I decided to talk to him one to one, as a friend.

The moment I raised this issue with him, he immediately replied with resentment: "Pratap, you don't know anything. You're too ignorant. You do not know how bad people are out there, you better be careful, you can be cheated easily."

People who knew him well used to say that he was so critical of everyone, that he could find fault even with God.

This doctor was good academically but because of his lack of Insight into his own life he was making himself, his family and people around him miserable.

You can surmise from the story that when one's critical nature becomes the dominating factor, it can make the person miserable. The unfortunate part is the person does not know what he/she is doing to him or herself. One may acquire this habit sometime in one's lifetime from any of the following reasons: poor upbringing, ego, or lack of insight into life and so on.

Secret #4. Anxiety and worry – One of the humans' worst enemies

I worry about everything; this is my nature. However, if there is nothing to worry about, I may get even more nervous, because now there is nothing left for me to do.
—Mrs. UP

As you know many people are the victims of anxiety and worries. Anxiety to a smaller degree and under certain stressful situations can be accepted as normal, and most people have experienced anxiety at one time or another. But this story that I am sharing with you is an extreme case.

Here is a dialogue between a patient and me from one of their office visits. You will see how anxiety is the key element in this case and how it is affecting the person negatively.

Dr. Singhal: Hello Mrs. UP, how are you?

Patient: I feel miserable.

Dr.: Why do you feel miserable?

Patient: Because I am worried about so many things.

Dr.: What are you worried about?

Patient: You will never understand that; just give me my anxiety medicine, and I hope that it will take care of it.

Dr.: Here is your prescription.

Patient: I can't read your handwriting; I don't understand why doctors write like this. Do you think the pharmacy will be able to read it?

Dr.: Yes, they know how to read it, and in case they can't, they will call me.

Patient: Do you think they have your phone number?

Dr.: Yes, look, it is at the top of the prescription.

Patient: If they call you, will you take their phone call?

Dr.: Yes, I do it all the time. This is my job.

Patient: I have noticed that your phone is always busy, how they can get in touch with you?

Dr.: They will try again and again, till they get me.

Patient: If I go to the pharmacy in the evening or weekend, how they will get hold of you?

Dr.: I have a 24-hour answering service.

Patient: Does your answering service know how to get hold of you?

Dr.: Yes, that's why I pay them.

Patient: Are you sure this medicine will work?

Dr.: I think so, however, if it does not, I will change it.

Patient: If it does not work, what will you give me next?

Dr.: I shall evaluate at that time.

Patient: And if the second medicine does not work, do you have other choices, or it is the end of my life?

Dr.: Do not worry, I have plenty of different medications to try.

Patient: If you go on vacation, what would I do?

Dr.: I have a covering doctor who will take care of you.

Patient: Does the covering doctor have access to my records in case you're not here?

Dr.: No, he does not have access to your records, but he knows what to do, and he can contact me through my cell phone.

Dear reader, this is typical of one visit with this patient. This is not a laughing matter, although it might make you laugh. At times, it can become very frustrating. The point I wish to make is that when anxiety and worry begin to control someone's life, you can never tell what is going on in the patient's mind and how he/she is suffering internally. The only thing that you can do is to just sympathize with them.

Anxiety and worry are one of the worst enemies of a person's happiness. They not only affect the life of the person negatively, but also of the family and friends around the patient.

Secret #5. Fear — the ghost

Fear, like any other negative element, can be very destructive, especially when it begins to control a person's life. It can take away all of a person's joy and happiness. To what degree a person will suffer depends on how much control fear has over them.

In my clinical practice, I often see a significant number of patients who have fears. Unfortunately, I see cases where people have multiple fears. But even worse is when people can't even explain what they're afraid of. They are simply terrified.

Fear can be of anything and everything. Here are a few examples of fears which people commonly suffer:

Fear of the dark.

Fear to go out.

Fear of driving.

Fear of starting a project, in case they fail.

Fear of taking an exam.

Fear of being criticized, therefore not offering one's opinion, or asking questions and staying ignorant.

Fear of being poisoned by a friend of the family. (Yes, it's true, I have seen cases.)

Fear of death.

Fear of disease, especially cancer.

Fear of germs.

Fear of the unknown.

You need to know that the list of the fears is endless.

Next, coming to the definition of the word fear, the Oxford English Dictionary defines fear as an unpleasant emotion caused by threat or danger, pain or harm. However, when I took classes in hypnosis, I learned a unique way of understanding the word fear. You know that the word "fear" has four letters, and each letter stands for something as follows:

F: false

E: evidence

A: appears

R: real

In my clinic when patients come to me with any kind of fears, I tell them, "Look, we all die one day and that is okay, but people with fear die on a daily basis. Which would you rather choose? It is all up to you!"

I believe that fear is the ghost of one's imagination. The ghost can take any size, shape or form and there is no limit to it. The more dangerous the size and shape of the fear a person can create in his or her imagination, the more the person suffers. When I think of how people suffer from their fears, sometime I wonder which is worse, fear or cancer.

Secret #6. Can anger make a person a devil?

I'm going to share two stories in this section. Let me begin with a story from my college days. One Saturday afternoon, I walked to the home of a classmate who lived just a couple of blocks away. The purpose of the visit was social, I was bored. This incident happened 50 years ago, when the phone was a scarcity. Everybody did not have a phone, nor did I. When I reached his home, I rang the doorbell and my friend came out. He told me, "Pratap, you better leave in a hurry, because Devil is home."

I got a little perplexed and nervous after he said this. I could not understand. I noticed stress and fear written on his face. Then I asked him what he meant. He replied, with emphasis, "Pratap, for now, please leave in a hurry, because Devil is home, and I shall explain to you more on Monday when I see you at college."

I turned around and start walking fast away from his home. I had not gone even 15 feet when his father came out of the house and called me back. His voice was loud and a little harsh. I could not decide whether I should go back or not. But I did anyway.

I stood in front of his father, a tall, heavyset middle-aged man with red eyes and big lips. I would call him at least obese to morbidly obese.

He started an interrogation with me, as if I was bothering his son or I was a bad person. He asked a million questions, which were hard for me to understand. I could not answer the baseless questions /accusations that he was throwing at me. He made me feel so bad that I almost cried. Finally, I left and was sad for the remainder of the weekend.

On Monday morning, my friend came to me and apologized deeply for his father's behavior. He was very upset but told me that he could not help. My friend also told me that everybody called his father a devil. "When he comes home from work, we children all run to our rooms, scared of him. Our mother is equally scared of him. When he yells at her, she trembles. Everybody prays that we don't get called by our father. Because whenever he calls anyone, usually the purpose is to yell and scream because he is always angry about something or other. Whenever one of us gets called by my father, all children pray for the welfare of their sibling. Even my mother does not speak a word when he is at home. My mother understands our situation and loves us dearly but she also feels helpless. And when my father goes to work, we all feel happy and relieved." Is it not sad, that children feel good when the father leaves, should it not be the other way around?

Of course, this is an extreme case. But there are many people in this world who suffer from anger to some degree or other. The unfortunate part is that these people do not realize how they are affecting their own lives and the lives of others.

Here is another story about anger. One of my aunts visited India from the USA to see her parents. It so happened that while in India she had to visit a doctor for some reason. Somehow or other, she was a little late for her appointment, which was not unusual for her, and the doctor got angry at her. She asked the doctor, "Why are you so mad for something so small." Thereafter the doctor became more furious.

In India, madness does not mean anger; it means that a person is crazy and needs psychiatric help. Whereas in the USA, the word "mad" is used in exchange for "angry." So, partially it is a question of cultural difference.

Yes, anger can make a person mad or devilish. The reason being that during the period of anger, that person loses him or herself and therefore could behave like a mad person. We are now learning that when people are angry all the time it has a long-term negative effect on the brain, including early dementia.

I wish to suggest that these two examples can be an opportunity for everyone to reflect on their own life and understand if anger is an element of their life. More importantly, if one can come up with a plan to take measures to reduce the same.

Let me say something about anger from the Scriptures. The difference between anger and fire is not that much. Except that fire is a physical element, and anger is a metaphysical element, and both can be very destructive.

Secret #7. How greed can destroy a family?

Here is an old story that happened more than 20 years ago, but is worth presenting here because of its instructional value. It is the story of a family which consists of two brothers and four sisters. The mother had died a long time ago. The youngest daughter named Ms. PR had been my patient for many years. She is 57 years old and has a history of minor arthritis, and some anxiety issues. She is quite an emotional person.

On each visit, she will brag about how good her family members are. The whole family gets together on every holiday, such as Thanksgiving, Christmas, and New Year's Eve. Not only this, everybody is close-knit and cares for each other dearly. Since Miss PR is quite an emotional person, I let her express her feelings, because I notice that when she talks about her family her heart is filled with joy and she gets emotional and tears up.

The story begins after the sudden death of her father. His will was read with all the family members present. To the surprise of my patient, she was the only one who was not named as a beneficiary, while everybody else was. It killed her emotionally. So, she expressed to her sisters that she was very saddened that their father did not name her as a beneficiary. In response, all the sisters replied in one tone, "Maybe our father did not want you to be the beneficiary. We do not know why, however, it is important that we must respect our father's wishes."

However, the two brothers did not like their sisters' answer, and they had a different way of thinking. They thought that they must get to the bottom of this, and there must be something wrong with the will, because their father was fair and just, and loved everybody equally. After analysis, they found out that the will was written long before the youngest sister was born, and unfortunately the father never updated it.

One week later both brothers called a family meeting, and presented their case: "Look, family, we are all here together. We are a close-knit family and let us keep it that way. We brothers have analyzed the situation and this is what we are presenting here to you.

"We have come to understand that the will was written long before our youngest sister was born and unfortunately it was never updated.

"Our father has left us $15,000 in total. If we split it equally, we will get $2500 each. However, if we do not let our youngest sister have her share, the rest of us will get $3000 each. So, it is a question of only $500 less per person.

"Since we are a close-knit family, we cannot break family bonds and values for the small sum of $500. Money should be a small issue when we are talking about family togetherness. Therefore, we both brothers are requesting that everyone write a check for $500 to our little sister and we all will be a happy family again, otherwise, there could be a long-term difference among family members."

At this juncture, the eldest sister spoke. "I do not agree with your plan. We must respect the wishes of our late father. Therefore, I am keeping my money, because that's what our father wanted."

Immediately thereafter, the second sister said the same thing. "I agree with the elder sister; we should respect the wishes of our father as it is written in the will. So, I am also going to keep my money."

The third sister finally spoke. "I cannot go against my other two sisters. I also must agree with my elder sisters. So, I am also going to keep my money."

The meeting ended in total disappointment for the brothers and the youngest sister. They could not tolerate her disappointment and her tears. Both brothers wrote a check for $500 each in her name and told her, "We are sorry but we have tried our best."

One month after this incident, Ms. PR came to my office and told me exactly what happened. She told me, "I am totally devastated by the behavior of my sisters. Now, none of the sisters will talk to me and they have alienated me." Her family was broken. She cried and told me further that "for a small amount of money, my sisters have lost all the love and relationship that we had for years. I have no family left. I was never married and I have no children. My family was everything to me. Now I am all alone. The way it looks I must spend my holidays and Christmas alone. I feel forsaken and neglected."

Can you imagine three sisters turning against their own youngest sister just for a small sum of $500? The small money versus the long-term family bonds? Such can be the power of greed.

Secret #8. The habit of comparing – the unfair and unethical game

You all know that the habit of comparing has no place in the civilized world, although this game is still being played by many Ignorant ones. The purpose behind this game is that a person is trying to show that he/she is superior than the other person. I believe that the person who plays this game are victim of superiority or even inferiority complex.

You also understand that this game is harmful not only to the person to whom it is directed, but also the person who plays this game.

Let me begin with why this game is bad and unfair. Firstly, it is hard to compare any two people, because no two people are alike, as there are so many variables. Secondly, it is easy to understand that there are always some people who are superior and others who are inferior in one or other qualities of life.

Finally, the outcome of this game is equally bad. For example, when a person compares him or herself with somebody inferior, it may be the cause of false uplift or ego. However, if the same person compares him or herself with somebody superior, it may be a cause of sadness and/or depression.

Let me show you by example, how people play this game. Say there are two people, A and B. Let us also presume that A and B are at the same level of life. And A has an inferiority complex and is playing.

A will compare him or herself with another person who is at a lower level and will falsely upgrade or prove that he or she is better. But then person A, will compare person B with someone who is on a higher level, trying to make the point that B is inferior.

This unethical game has no place in society.

Secret #9. Complaining — a nasty habit

Mrs. NSC came to me five years ago. This was my first encounter with her. She was referred to me by a doctor friend who wanted me to use hypnosis for her condition. I introduced myself and asked her, "How are you and how can I help?"

Asking this question was, like opening a Pandora's box. The moment I asked, she started talking. She said, "I feel miserable. I have so much to tell you I do not know where to start. But I can tell you that nobody has been able to help me, including my doctor. Therefore, he has asked me to take your advice. I hope you can help."

I told her, "Go ahead, I am ready to listen." Before I could finish my sentence, she opened her notebook, which contained pages and pages of complaints. This book was very old and falling apart and it appeared that it had been read hundreds of times before.

She asked me, "Please let me read from my book, otherwise, I am afraid that I will miss something." Thereafter she started to tell her story.

After listening for 10 minutes to her story and list of complaints, I told her, "Let us take a pause. Let me try to understand what you're trying to say." She interrupted, saying that she was not finished yet, and there was much more that she must tell me.

I said "Yes, I understand that, but we must take a pause before going any further." After hearing her complaints, I could understand that they had no logic. My doctor friend had warned me that she did not listen and just talked.

Further, I realized that her complaints go back at least 20 years or more, to when she got married. At least 30% of the complaints were about her husband and another 30% about her mother-in-law. This was just the beginning. She had complaints about her neighbor, their barking dog which did not let her sleep, her sisters who didn't care about her, her children who didn't listen to her, and the damp weather in the area where she lived which affected her asthma.

While I was still interviewing her, I was interrupted by a phone call from her husband who told me, "Dr. Singhal, please help her and us, because not only she is miserable but she makes everybody around her miserable. Her mother and her younger sister have a similar history, maybe it is in the genes."

The purpose of the story is not to show you how I helped her, but to demonstrate to you how people make themselves and others miserable by their complaining nature. Of course, it maybe be justifiable if the complaint has a basis and person is seeking a solution. However, that was not her motive, she just wanted somebody to listen to her complaints.

Nowadays people have become wiser. Ever since I started my medical practice, I have noticed that the number of the people who complain is getting smaller each year. These days, people are coming to the realization that complaining is bad and useless for everyone, including the person who complains. You also know that most people do not pay attention to the complaints of others and say it is nonsense chatter, whereas other, wiser people often remark "Why complain, nobody listens." Which is of course true. They often further add:

Everybody has enough problems and complaints of their own, and then how they will find the time to listen to the complaints of others?

It is equally important to understand that people who are in the habit of complaining turn off other people, and other people learn to avoid them. This is also called "the behavior of avoidance." I have discussed this subject in this very section, in one of the upcoming stories.

In essence, complaining is bad, nonproductive and a fruitless habit, and it is full of negativity. It can make the person and the people around him or her miserable. People learn to avoid the company of such people. I also want to draw your attention to the fact that although the number of people who complain persistently is getting smaller, there are still people who waste their precious time this way.

I believe there is a clear difference between how the happy and unhappy people think. The unhappy one focus on the problems, and the happy one on the solution.

Secret #10. When people let traffic (or anything else) control their lives

Traffic is an everyday problem and affects everyone to some degree or other. But when people get overwhelmed by it, they become the victim and thus suffer.

One of my patients, named Miss VT, came to me for her regular checkup one Monday morning. She was upset and looked exhausted and told me, "Dr. Singhal, maybe we should postpone today's physical for some other day because I had a rough weekend, so my blood pressure must be high."

I said, "Sure, as you wish, it is all up to you. But please tell me what happened?"

She said, "Last weekend, I went to see one of my best friends who lives 79 miles away. It was a Friday evening and the traffic was crazy. The highway was packed and it was like a parking lot. To make things worse it was raining and freezing cold so the roads were kind of slippery. It took me three and a half hours to get to my friend's home, when normally I can make it in an hour and a half. When I reached my friend's home, I was exhausted. I could not enjoy Friday evening, and I went to sleep. I woke up fresh on Saturday morning and had a good weekend with my friend.

"On my way back, it was another story. It was Sunday afternoon and the traffic were heavy again. The weather was nice. People were driving 70 to 80 mph. They were passing me right and left. I do not care when people pass but what bothered me was when people came up behind my car and started honking at me because they wanted me to pull to the side. That made me so angry, I was ready to cry. Last night, I got home around nine PM, but I was so upset and angry that I could not fall asleep. I think that must have raised my blood pressure."

I asked her, "Can I give you advice?" She said sure. I told her, "Look, when you travel you should try to use your time for something useful such as listening to music or any audio program that you subscribe to for any purpose. That way you will never feel the stress of traffic, and you will not feel that you are wasting your time. Secondly, when people honk at you, you need to know that they have no right to push you to the side of the road."

Next, I asked her, "Do you know what I do in those cases?"

She replied, "Please tell me."

I told her, "If somebody does that to me, I take charge of the situation. I don't let the driver of the car in the back control me. Neither do I change my lane, nor go any faster. As a matter of fact, I do the opposite. I start to slow down till the person behind me changes his or her lane out of frustration. And after they pass me, I return to the speed I was driving before. I believe that changing the lane is their problem and not yours. You must remember that." She just smiled.

We all know that traffic is not going to go away. Therefore, it is important to develop a strategy to deal with these problems. This story has another important message: that one should not let anything control his/her life. Being controlled by someone means being the victim, that translates into pain or suffering.

Secret #11. How to deal with unpleasant, nasty or difficult people

In my school days, I had to walk half a mile from home to school in the morning and back home in the evening. But there was a shop on my route that I always had to pass which I did not like. The owner of the shop was a very old man. I believe he did not like children. Either he used to say nasty things to me and other children or used to scare them.

Whenever I was approaching the shop, I used to peek carefully from a distance, to see whether the old man was there. When he was not there, I felt relieved and walked comfortably past his shop. However, when he was there, I used to just run past quickly, to minimize the exposure time to that person. It was really bad in the sense that I had to deal with it at least twice a day.

One day I told my father about it. He told me that he knew the old man and he was crazy. He also advised me not to take that route again. What a simple solution to a big problem for me at that age! Although now I had to walk extra 50 to 75 feet every time. I like to call this "the behavior of avoidance."

The incident I have described was a simple case. However, many times we must deal with unpleasant people or even difficult ones, especially those whom we can't avoid that easily: a difficult boss, a spouse, a friend, or a relative. This technique of avoidance can be used by anyone; however, one must develop his/her own strategy. Let me give you a concrete example.

One of my patients came to me and told me that she was a happy woman, however, her coworker was a very negative person and drained her energy with constant negative chatter. I told her my story and advised her that she could also use that technique of avoidance, but she had to develop her own strategy.

I saw the patient again after two months and she was very happy. She told me that she had been using the technique that I had given her last time and it was working wonderfully. I asked her to explain how she did it.

She replied, "As you know, I clean houses for a living. Before I came to you, I used to work as part of a two-person team on one job, then move to the second one and so on. However, now we split the jobs into two. She takes one job and I take the other. This way I don't see her much. Not only this, when we go for lunch I either go for a walk or pretend to sleep, so that I don't have to spend much time with her. This has made a tremendous difference in my life, and now I am happy again."

You can appreciate from this that you can also work out a plan or a strategy based on your situation. I have personally used myself this technique several times in my life. The behavior of avoidance can be a boon to anyone who needs it. Of course, one must come up with his/her own strategy based on the situation.

Secret #12. Shoplifting — its never-ending curse

Once a lady came to me very depressed. She told me that it was very frustrating and depressing that she could not find a job. She had been looking for 10 years. I asked her why she couldn't find a job.

She replied, "Ten years ago, I used to work for a store and at one time I was caught shoplifting, and they immediately fired me. Now, whenever I go for a new job, while filling out the application I must answer the question as to why I left the last job. And I have been telling the truth. After the interview, they say they will get back to me. But I never hear from them."

She continued, "Once I managed to get a job by lying on the application. I worked very hard at this job with loyalty and sincerity to wash off my past bad karma. I was very happy, and three and a half years went by. But a previous customer came to the shop who knew me, and out of jealousy, she told my boss about my history of shoplifting. My boss immediately fired me. Not only this, I was accused of taking all the items missing from the shop, of which I had no knowledge. My boss also refused to pay me my last two weeks of salary."

At this juncture, I suggested to my patient that maybe she should start her own small business. She replied that it was not possible, because she had neither the money nor any skills. What a sad story!

Shoplifting, like any other similar negative quality, can become a curse in a person's life. There are at least two reasons for that: firstly, that bad habits are hard to break and secondly, the effects of such habits may be hard to wash off. Of course, the best solution is prevention. Good habits are best learned during early life by inculcating good human values. This requires hard work and discipline, but you cannot match the benefits of those values.

Section Three

The Fourteen amazing Tenets of the "Law of Nothingness"

The 'Law of Nothingness' is my own formulation. I have coined this law initially however, very briefly in my first book in 2010 — Health, Happiness and You---Everything You Need to Know, in the chapter The Art of happiness.

What is the source of the law of nothingness? The law of nothingness (and its 14 tenets) is the product of my own meta-analysis of life experiences, and study of the Scriptures.

A word about the Scriptures: The Scriptures are the 1st book ever created on this universe. I called them the manuals of life. They are written for the well-being and happiness of all. You need to know that they are the 1st ever book came into existence. All present knowledge is an offshoot of them.

In this section, I shall discuss the fourteen tenets of the "law of nothingness." I will say from the very beginning that these 14 tenets are so powerful that, when understood and practiced in real life, they can make a vast difference in raising your happiness level. These have been a boon to my life, and I hope they can also be to yours.

What is the key message of the "law of nothingness"? Relax, enjoy and be happy, everywhere, every time and in all situations. Because at the end of the day everything will be fine. So why to stress, and not just enjoy?

I believe this law is very timely because today everybody lives in distress. Life is too busy and demanding, and most people have no time to relax. Going one step further, this law also has a positive connotation. In my opinion it is another path to happiness. Therefore, it is the need of the moment.

I must comment that the above message is very powerful and is based upon hardcore truth. However, it requires little time and wisdom to assimilate the information it contains. But once you understand this hardcore truth, your life can change for the better and happiness will come home in no time.

What was the triggering factor that led to the formulation of the law of nothingness? An insight and reflection into life! I have been searching to understand why there has been so much unhappiness, restlessness, sadness, suffering and negativity in this world despite all the goodness that exists here. What really struck me most was this passage from the Bhagavad-Gita:

Everything in life is good, everything that is happening is good, everything that will happen will also be good, and in the end everything will be good.

Before going any further, I must comment on the word "nothingness". Nothingness does not mean zero, but it implies something insignificant. For example, you must have noticed in daily life that when you ask a person what they're doing, and if they are not doing anything important, they will often reply "Nothing, I was just watching TV," or looking at the newspaper or whatever.

Before getting deeper into this section, I must make some comments about Murphy's Law, which has some relationship to the law of nothingness. Murphy's Law states, "If anything can go wrong, it will." So, in a way it may look contrary to the law of nothingness, but that is not the case.

Although Murphy's Law is well intended, and prepares a person for the worst, at the same time, it may have a negative connotation at least to the mind of some.

Here are the 14 tenets of the law of nothingness. Please note that the first five are simple and easy to understand. But the remaining nine tenets have deeper meaning and are more powerful.

Tenet #1. You come with nothing.

Tenet #2. You will go with nothing.

Tenet #3. Assume nothing.

Tenet #4. Presume nothing.

Tenet #5. Judge nothing.

Tenet #6. Expect nothing.

Tenet #7. There is nothing so good in life that you should feel that you have won the lottery.

Tenet #8. There is nothing as bad as you may think. Everything has a positive and negative side to it. However, you have to think deeply to get the global picture.

Tenet #9. If you keep thinking about an idea or subject for long enough, you can create something from nothing.

Tenet #10. An ignorant person can make a mountain of nothing, whereas a wise person can convert a mountain into nothing.

Tenet #11. Fear nothing.

Tenet #12. There is nothing in the world the loss of which should make you cry, at least not for long.

Tenet #13. Your life is the most precious thing, so there's nothing worth getting attached or bonded to.

Tenet #14. You need nothing more than you already have to be happy.

There is an additional bonus secret that has been slightly modified by me, that is:

'Nothing belongs to you and you belong to nothing.'

For the explanation and modification see the detailed explanation of the Tenets.

Next, let me expand on each of the 14 tenets in detail. I also called them the 14 secrets.

Secret/Tenet #1: You come with nothing.

Remember, when you landed on this earth, you came with nothing. The only thing you brought with you was your soul and the karmas of your past. You did not have any clothes on you. Your body was also given to you by your mother. Since you did not bring anything with you onto this earth, therefore nothing is yours, including this body.

However, you could say that you may have brought some happiness to your parents, but only after you made several good cries.

Here I wish to remind you that each of the tenets conveys a special meaning. So, please give due thought to each of the tenets before moving to the next one.

Secret/Tenet # 2: You will go with nothing.

Have you ever seen anybody taking away anything from this earth when they leave? You can reflect on the life of people long gone. It could be your friends, relatives, the mighty kings, even your own ancestors. You can be sure that you will also not take anything from here.

You would not be able to take even your dear ones with you, the reason being that in reality they do not belong to you. It is only because of circumstances that they have become your friend, relative, or acquaintance.

So, the only elements that you're going to take with you are your own soul and your karma, because that is your real property. This is what you brought with you, and this is what will go with you.

However, if you believe in reincarnation, you know that these elements — your mind and your karma — will stay with you for all your future lives.

Since you are the soul, and the soul is the most precious element of life that any human being can have, yet some people inadvertently cause damage to their souls by wrongful acts such as cheating, deceiving or harming others. If you have read the Scriptures, you must have read that many great prophets call this life a drama or illusion, because once life is over, everything is over.

Next let me say something about the wisdom of Mother Earth. She is very wise and possessive of her elements. She will not let you take anything from her. I think she believes that you are a guest on this earth. She wants you to enjoy your stay and expects that when you leave, you will leave the planet the way you came. Which is quite fair. Of course, if you want to make Mother Earth happy, then make this a better place than before you came in.

There is another reason that Mother Earth does not want to take anything from here — because she wants to protect and preserve the land so that the coming generation can also enjoy it. She is smart enough to know that if everybody will take away just one thing from here, soon she will be empty.

One needs to know that Mother Earth has already served more than one hundred billion people in the past since the time of creation, although the population of the world at the time of writing this book is only seven billion. Thus, the tenet "you go with nothing" has a powerful and practical truth.

Secret/Tenet #3: Assume nothing.

The word assume means to accept something as truth without proof. Some people like to call it jumping to a conclusion based on hearsay.

Have you ever given a thought to how bad it could be to assume something without any proof? Let me give you a concrete example. Somebody comes in and tells you that your dearest friend does not like you, or even hates you. And based on this hearsay, you assume that your friend talks bad about you.

Without giving due consideration to what you have heard, you call your best friend and start yelling at him. You tell him what you have heard, without even giving him a chance to explain. But later you realize that the information was wrong; you were misled, and it is too late. Before you know it, your friendship is over and you have a lost a lifetime good friend. This is what assumption can do to you. Is it not sad?

Therefore, please be aware that assumptions can have serious consequences. Also, more often than not, one can make a fool of him or herself in the end.

Secret/Tenet #4. Presume nothing.

The word presume means to take something for granted, based upon probability.

You know the word probability is not the same as reality. Probability is far away from the reality. You can say it falls between the possibility and the reality. Let me give you the sequence: Possibility > probability > reality.

Next let me give you a concrete example, from my own experience, that has taught me an important lesson.

Three years ago, I was to give a presentation at 9 AM at the yearly meeting. It was a very important meeting. I arrived at 8:45 AM, 15 minutes before the scheduled time. I had presumed that my room for presentation would be ready including equipment and set up. However, that did not happen, as it used to happen in the past, so my presumption was wrong.

At that point, the only choice I had was either to yell and scream and kill myself or just go to the director and ask for help. And that was what I did. What I learned was that the person who had initially been assigned to set up my room was given another duty by mistake. The director apologized and sent me another helper and we set up the room for the presentation. But everything was delayed by 20 minutes.

I kept my anger and frustration to myself, but that took lots of energy out of me. I gave my presentation and did my best not to show it to the audience. But I could feel inside that I was not normal. Of course, I could not blame the person and certainly not the director of the program. So, the only person to suffer was me. Still, something very good came out of it — I learned a life lesson: not to presume ever again.

This incident made me smarter. Not so bad after all! We all learn from our mistakes. Now I go at least one hour early and make sure that everything is set properly. Most of you may have been in a similar situation in your life. It is an opportunity to reflect on those times and learn from them.

Secret/Tenet #5. Judge nothing.

We are not the judges. You, me or anyone else. Judgment is given by God only. He is the highest judge of all and the final one.

Of course, there are judges in the court system; that is a totally different issue. You may know that even judges on occasion make gross mistakes and hang up the innocent, because they are only human. Nobody can blame them, because they have a system that they must follow, which is based on the evidence presented. On many occasions the truth does not come out, and the innocent are punished.

I'm sure you would be interested to know how a judge thinks. Once I was having a social conversation with a wise judge. I told him that judges are the providers of justice in the court. In response, he replied, "I do not know whether you call it justice or injustice. The party that wins calls it justice and the other party that loses, calls it an injustice."

Making judgments about others is not humane. Society does not like it and the Scriptures condemn it. People who make judgments about others are ignorant and lack insight of their own shortcomings. You must also have noticed that when a person gives a negative judgment about others, more often than not, they get into trouble.

Next, I would like to remind you that, from now on each tenet becomes more and more powerful and hence requires closer attention.

Secret/Tenet #6. Expect nothing.

I can say from experience that expectation and miseries are directly and proportionately related. The higher the expectation, the greater the misery.

The *Bhagavad-Gita* has stated so beautifully in the following words: *Do your duty, for the sake of duty.*

(In other words, do not expect any return, because when you expect something you may be looking for sadness or pain.)

This is a tough principle to follow. At times the teaching of Scripture is hard to assimilate, or even understand, however, it is based on wisdom.

Let me give you some concrete examples:

A child does not get the toy he expects on his birthday and throws a tantrum.

A student does not get the grade that he or she expects, and gets sad and frustrated.

A child does not get the expected share of the estate from his/her parents, or his or her sibling gets more than him or her. You can appreciate the anger and sense of jealousy.

A tired husband, who has a bad day at work, comes home dragging with the expectation of relief, but his wife is standing at the door with bad news. Or she sends him away for an important chore.

At a graduation ceremony, the keynote speaker does not show up on time.

You order a dress for an important event, to be ready at a certain time. You go there one hour early and the dress is not ready.

You are given a hard assignment for the weekend, but when Monday comes, you get a negative review.

These are only some real-life examples. Of course, there is no end to it.

Expectation and miseries are directly and proportionally related. If you sincerely want happiness, then stop expecting anything and from anyone. However, you should continue to expect yourself to be better and stronger each day in every way.

After reading this tenet, you can probably appreciate more the power and the message of the *Bhagavad-Gita*, i.e. *Do your duty for the sake of duty*.

Secret/Tenet #7. There is nothing so good in life, that you should feel that you have won the lottery.

There are two reasons for this. Firstly, everything in life is transient, and secondly, the importance and the significance of everything decreases with time. However, it requires a little insight to appreciate that.

Let me give you a concrete example from my own experience. When I became a doctor, I was jumping up and down in my heart as if I had won the lottery. But when I went to my first job interview, I realized that real life is not easy for anyone, and professionals are no exception.

Let me give you a few more examples to clarify my point. Let us take the dress issue. This is especially common in girls. They pick up a very special dress about which they are crazy. They wear it once, twice or a few times and they get tired of it.

Say you buy a dress with your full heart in it and it takes only one person to say this dress does not look good on you, this changes the whole picture, and now you're not so sure if this was a good choice.

Finally, it is not uncommon these days that people date for years to find the best partner, and finally, they become crazy for each other and get married. As soon as they get married, they start finding fault with each other and become unhappy or even miserable. Before you know they are in divorce court.

The wise tell us that, in life nothing is one hundred percent good, or bad. Everything has a positive or a negative side. However, it requires insight to appreciate the total picture. The fact is that the people who can see through the whole picture don't get overwhelmed easily with positivity or even negativity. That is one of the great achievements towards the goal of happiness.

Secret/Tenet #8. There is nothing as bad as you think.

This reminds me one of the words of Shakespeare: *there is nothing either good or bad, but thinking makes it so.*

It is true that everything in life has a positive and negative aspect to it. There are no exceptions to this. The problem is that people who are negative usually stay more focused on the negative side and can't look at the positive side and thus suffer. Of course, it is equally true that people who are always positive often fail to understand the negative side of elements and therefore do not get the complete picture. That is not good either. In life one has to be realistic. Neither very pessimistic nor very optimistic.

Here are some examples:

One of my professors in medical school never hesitated to fail a student if they did not do extremely well in her opinion. One time she was asked why she failed so many students. Her reply was, being a doctor is a great thing. The doctor must deal with the lives of the people. So, if I fail a student, the worst thing that can happen is that the student must study six months extra, but that will make him/her a much better doctor. She used to say that the passing grades set by the universities were not good enough.

(This was her point of view, which I am not condoning.)

Let me give you another example. Three years after my graduation I became very sick in the hospital because of a kidney stone. Unfortunately, or fortunately, no medicine was helping me. I was going from bad to worse. I was getting frustrated with my sickness and the medical system that was not helping me. Then came a big change in my life.

Just at that time, one of the great homeopaths came into my life and cured me in less than 10 minutes. After I got better with the homeopathic medicine, my life was totally transformed for the better. Today I feel lucky because that sickness has expanded my vision. Since then I have incorporated homeopathic and other complementary medical sciences into my practice, and therefore I can help many more patients in a much better way.

Before this incident, I used to think that the conventional medical science was the best and complete, and of course, I was wrong. No medical science is complete. All are complementary and have something to offer, and at times can fill the gap that another has left.

In life, nothing is one hundred percent bad, many bad times often bring goodness or even an opportunity for betterment.

Secret/Tenet #9. If you keep thinking about an idea or subject for long enough, you can create something from nothing.

The fact of the matter is, we see very little of anything, or you can say that we see things very superficially. In fact, everything is much deeper than an average person thinks. Every object and idea have a deeper meaning and roots, when you analyze them thoroughly.

Also, when you think about something at a deeper level, you will see that thing in several dimensions. Even if you look at an average person, he or she is much deeper than you can imagine. I am saying this based upon my experience by having deep conversations and listening to average people.

That is how many thinkers and philosophers have come up with ideas and hypothesis. Sometimes it appears that the solution was already hanging in the air, and they just caught it and presented it to the world.

Let me give you a concrete example. You have seen several times an apple falling from a tree. What a simple thing! How many millions of people had observed that? I'll bet that even Sir Isaac Newton himself must have observed apples falling from trees hundreds of times. It was a special day when he started questioning to himself why the apple fell from the tree, and it was that process that led to the discovery of the law of gravity. So, you can appreciate how deep and long thinking can become very creative.

(Per Scriptures, there are some flaws to the Newton law of gravity; however, that is not the point of discussion here, so I will leave it at that for now.)

Everybody has a little Isaac Newton in them. I believe when anybody can take time to think deeply and long enough on any subject, they can come up with some new idea or discovery.

Secret/Tenet #10. The ignorant person can make a mountain of nothing, whereas a wise person can convert a mountain into nothing.

You must have noticed that many simple/naïve people get very easily distressed by simple issues which are not even worth mentioning. The reason is, they stay focused on the problem so much and for so long that they forget to look for the solution. Whereas when a wise person faces a problem, his immediate attention goes to the cause and/or the solution. And as soon as he finds the solution, he just smiles.

The ignorant and wise have two different way of approaching a problem. One focuses on the problem and the other on the solution.

Secret/Tenet #11. Fear nothing.

I have discussed this topic in section two of this book, when talking about how to learn from unhappy people. Therefore, I will not dwell on it for long here. The only message I wish to repeat here is, whenever I come across a person who is fearful, I tell them: Every human being must die once, and that is okay. But people with the fear die on a daily basis. Which would you rather choose? It is your call!

Fear is like a ghost. Just turn on the light and the ghost will disappear.

Secret/Tenet #12. There is nothing in the world the loss of which should make you cry, at least not for long.

This is because of the following fact: Everything in this universe is of transient nature, and there's nothing which is permanent. This is equally applicable to you and me.

It is true that in this life you will lose and gain here and there. This is part of life. Nobody knows how much and when. Thank God for that. However, it can be predicted with accuracy that at the end everybody will be okay. So, it is better to enjoy and relax whenever you can.

Secret/Tenet #13. Remember that your life is the most precious element, so there's nothing more worth getting attached or bonded to.

When people get bonded or attached to anything, it can become a cause of suffering. The reason being that when you attach to something, you begin to identify yourself with that element or even the person or the organization. You also need to know that the attachment or bonding can be to anything, for example money, a house, an organization or even one's dear ones. But the real fact is that you are a divine human being, free and immortal.

Think about it.

For your information, I have narrated two stories of attachment versus nonattachment in the first section of this book and you can read those again if you so choose.

Bondage or attachment can become a cause of misery and suffering. Meditate about it.

Secret/Tenet #14. You need nothing more than you already have to be happy. All you have to do is make up your mind, or just choose happiness.

This point has been also stressed by his Holiness the Dalai Lama, in his book *The Art of Happiness*. I agree with that statement wholeheartedly.

The real fact is that happiness is not in the outer world but within oneself. Therefore, one should focus on the inner self, on strengthening and connecting with it. And when that happens, one will find happiness in no time, because the inner self is the seat of all happiness. Mahatma Buddha and many seers have come to the same conclusion.

The bonus tenet: Nothing belongs to you and you belong to Nothing.

This is slightly modified, please see the explanation below:

I am quoting the following statement of a great guru and Yogi — Lahiri Mahasaya, from the book *Autobiography of a Yogi* by Parmahansa Yogananda. On page 361 it states:

'Remember that you belong to no one and no one belongs to you. Reflect that someday you will suddenly have to leave everything in this world so make the acquaintance of God now.'

If I could rephrase the above statement in my own words, as an addition to the law of nothingness, I would write it as follows:

'Nothing belongs to you and you belong to nothing'.

Section Four

The Last Amazing Secret: Choose and Act

I have been saving this secret for the last, because it is extremely important. You can call it fine-tuning, the icing on the cake, or a dessert after a meal. So, what is the secret?

Remember I said in the very beginning of this book,

"Choose what you want and you will get what you choose."

You also know that choosing is only good when you act upon it. Because nothing happens without action. Action is the king.

Look deep into your own life and your successful points, you will agree that your success points are because you took action. You can also study the life of any great human being and you can realize that they became great only after they took action. No knowledge or idea is worth anything unless it is acted upon.

My friend, you have read at least 83 stories/secrets in this book. I believe you must have related your life experiences with at least few or maybe even many of them. Some stories might have touched your heart while others must have inspired you to take action. I recommend you read those stories again and again for the best benefit. I also firmly believe that now you're ready for action. Let me reiterate again that nothing happens without action and there is no better time than now for that.

To further inspire you and remind you of your mission on a daily basis, I have written this poem.

> My friend, it is all up to you,
>
> and all about you,
>
> you are the creator and in- charge
>
> of your life and of your world.
>
> It is only your thoughts and actions
>
> that determines who you are,
>
> and who you will be.
>
> Whether you will make this life
>
> happy or even miserable
>
> will depend on you.
>
> Because it is only up to you,
>
> and all about you.
>
> Remember, nobody is
>
> more powerful than you in this matter,
>
> because you are the creator of your life,
>
> and of your happy world.

Let me say once again,

it is all up to you

and all about you.

Finally, let me repeat the statement that I started with, in the very beginning of the book:

You choose what you want;

you will get what you choose.

APPENDIX
The Art of Happiness

The Art of Eternal Happiness: Always Calm, Always Happy

I have borrowed this article from one of my previous writings. I have slightly modified it for the sake of simplicity. I believe it will add further to your happiness. I hope you will enjoy and benefit from it.

Let me first define what is meant by eternal happiness: it means to be happy or at least staying balanced in all conditions and situations of life, whether it is positive or negative such as health or disease, pleasure or pain, gain or loss, etc.

Is it possible to be happy and/or balanced in most situations? Yes, it is for people like you and the wise. Because a wise person understands that ups and downs are part of every life and he or she is not a special being. Further, it becomes clear to him or her that all life situations and challenges are transient in nature, whereas a person is strong, brave, firm, and is here for a long time to come.

Before getting into the discussion let me clarify how eternal happiness differs from smiling, laughing, slaphappy, giggling, being "happy as a clam," etc. All these terms denote only short-term happiness and are transitory and conditional in nature, and are very different from eternal happiness. Those conditions do not have a solid footing.

Happiness is defined as a feeling of strong pleasure and contentment, or willingness to do and accept anything, or being fortunate and lucky. Let me say a few words about the importance of happiness:

Happiness is the need, desire and want of every human being. As a matter of fact, we do everything in life for the purpose of happiness. If you take that a step further, it is also the blessing of our parents, elders, gurus; even the Constitution of the United States of America is written for the freedom and happiness of all.

I have come to a realization in the mature years of my life that any person who is not happy in life should not consider him or herself a successful person, irrespective of what else he or she may have attained in the form of education, college degrees, wealth, family status, and social status, etc. Such is the importance of happiness.

You should also know that happiness cannot be linked to wealth, education, social status, or anything else because you shall find happy people in all walks of life. For example, some poor people are happy and others sad. Some educated people are happy and others sad. Some wealthy people are happy and others sad, and so on.

Swami Dayanand Saraswati, a guru, was the greatest humanitarian of his time. One day he was asked by the people why he worked so hard for the wellbeing of the society that he had no time to take care of himself. He replied, "The mission of my life is that I want freedom and happiness for the whole of humanity and not just for myself." You can appreciate from that how much importance the great swami has given to happiness.

The Vedas state that happiness is the prerequisite for salvation. According to these scriptures, each and every person without exception has to face difficulties and challenges in life, because these are part of normal life. Those who are mentally and spiritually strong can face the problems and difficulties in a calm and balanced manner and become victorious. They do not become victims of the problems of life; hence they find freedom, happiness, and finally salvation.

Please note that health and happiness are related and allied words. They vary in degree and/or intensity. Health means sound physical and mental condition, whereas happiness means sound physical and mental health, plus contentment and adeptness. The last two words, contentment and adeptness, are added to the definition of health and are the prerequisite for happiness.

I like to quote His Holiness the Dalai Lama in this area: "Today you have all the ingredients of happiness. You don't need a better career, a better wife, more money, better job, or better opportunities. You have everything right now, at this minute to be eternally happy."

In other words, happiness can be ours today without any change in the external world. Happiness lies within the heart and soul of every being; the only thing required of you is to peek within.

Why do we seek happiness? Simply because we miss it, because at one time we had it. We have been sidetracked and now we want to get back to where we belonged. Most people when they think of their earlier life and childhood, get the feeling of nostalgia. We also have come to the realization that we have been sidetracked and now it is a time to get back on the track so that we can enjoy the happiness again.

Let us begin the study of happiness in details. It will be discussed in four parts. First, we will study and learn from the behavior and characteristics of happy people. Second, we will study the behavior and characteristics of unhappy people and learn what led them into trouble or unhappiness, so that we do not fall into the same trap. Thirdly, we will compare and contrast the two for a better understanding. And finally, we do a meta-analysis of the subject.

Firstly, study of the characteristics and behavior of happy people: On a personal level, they usually:

Have a balanced state of mind.

Are calm by nature.

Have deep contentment in life.

Are at peace with the self.

Have good analytical ability and foresight.

Have an appreciation of life.

Have an ability to enjoy life as it is (without any precondition).

Accept life and its events as temporary and natural.

Have higher or highest goals or mission.

Have a good listening ability.

Appreciate the fact that opposing conditions and situations such as health and disease, pain and pleasure, success and failure, honor and insult, birth and death, are part of life.

On an interpersonal level, they:

Work on getting rid of the ego.

Are pleasant to deal with.

Have a comforting and helpful nature.

Have love and compassion for others.

Next, let us analyze the characteristics and behavior of unhappy people. On a personal level, they usually:

Have an unbalanced state of mind.

Have wandering minds.

Are restless and impatient.

Are poor listeners and have short fuses?

Are shortsighted.

Complain about and are discontented with life, people, possessions and situations.

Have lower goals and ambitions.

Are unable to enjoy life, as if they are waiting for something good to happen.

Feel like they are a victim of every misfortune in life, e.g., pain suffering, illness, etc.

Are ignorant about life, e.g., they do not understand life and have poor analytic ability

On an interpersonal level, they:

Have imbalanced egos, either feeling very special or at the bottom.

Are unpleasant and unpredictable in their dealings and behavior.

Are selfish in nature (a telltale sign) and are here only for themselves.

Thirdly, compare and contrast the differences between the behavior and characteristics of happy and unhappy people for better understanding.

Happy People = HP   Unhappy People= UNP

Upbringing

HP – Usually good upbringing

UNP – May have poor upbringing

Art and Science

HP – Constantly searching for happiness

UNP – No such vision; lack insight.

Seat of happiness

HP – Know that happiness lies in the heart and soul, not outside

UNP – Look for happiness in the wrong places and the wrong things, i.e., money, position, power, spouse, and family

Focus

HP – Focus on positive events, people and aspects of life

UNP – Focus on negative events, people, and aspects of life

Mind

HP – Healthy and balanced state of mind

UNP – Flickering and unstable state of mind

Energy

HP – Positive energy and positive aura

UNP – Negative energy and no aura

Behavior

HP – Pleasant to talk to, predictable behavior

UNP – Moody; unpredictable behavior

Appreciation

HP – Appreciate everything they have

UNP – Do not appreciate what they have, rather complain about everything they could have.

Contentment

HP – Content and satisfied with what they have

UNP – Neither content nor satisfied, no matter what they may have, because they want more and more

Complaining

HP – Usually do not complain about anything, and accept people and situations as they are

UNP – Complain about everything, including their job, the weather, their spouse, their friends and families and so on

Equal Rights

HP – Believe in equal rights

UNP – Do not have this concept

Opinion

HP – Respect their opinions, as well as those of others

UNP – Dogmatic and force their views on others/or may even downgrade others' viewpoint

Success and Failure

HP – there is nothing like failure, if they fail try again.

UNP – if there is a failure, it is all over.

Interdependence

HP – Believe and understand we need each other and are interdependent

UNP – Believe people need them, or even feel that they are dependent upon others

Altruism

HP – Respect and care for others

UNP – Selfish and indifferent to others

Acceptance

HP – they avoid arguments and are open-minded

UNP – Argue and easily get into fights, because do not know how to accept others' point of view

Life Outlook

HP – See life as challenging, but make the best of it; it has roses and thorns

UNP – Life is pain, suffering, and thorns

Anxiety and Worry

HP – Don't worry about anything unnecessarily

UNP – Spend so much time in anxiety and worry that hardly any time is left for anything else

Fault-Finding

HP – Focused on and strive for continuous improvement for a happier life

UNP – Focused on weaknesses of theirs as well as of others, with no clue or efforts on improving

Take Responsibility

HP – Take responsibility for whatever happens, good and bad

UNP – Blame others for any misfortune or negative outcome

Truth

HP – Tell the truth

UNP – Lie and keep secrets

Ego

HP – Give up their ego, everyone is equal without exception. We are just numbers.

UNP – Have problems with their ego, think they are very special and indispensable, or on the contrary, believe they are not worthy of anything

Expectation

HP – Don't expect anything from anybody, expect from the self

UNP – Expect too much from others, often a cause of anger and frustration

Dependency

HP – Do not depend upon others

UNP – Depend so much upon others, that it can become a cause of failure

Life's View

HP – Have good understanding and insight into life

UNP – Lack insight into life

Results and Methods

HP – Focus on the right path, and not so much on the results/outcomes

UNP – More focused on results, and not on right or wrong

Focus

HP – Focus on solving the problems

UHP – Focus on counting the problems and the difficulties.

Finally, a meta-analysis of Happiness and unhappiness: in four parts

Causes of unhappiness.

Test – Are you a happy person?

On the scale of happiness, where would you fit?

A true story

Unhappiness is based on diseases and/or weaknesses at the physical, mental, and spiritual levels. Most people may be aware of only physical diseases or weaknesses, and may not have understanding of mental and spiritual diseases. In truth, it is the latter that are the main causes of misery and unhappiness. I have listed physical, mental and spiritual diseases in three columns below, for better understanding:

Physical level	Mental level	Spiritual level
Diabetes	Sleeplessness	Selfishness
Arthritis	Depression	Lack insight into life
Asthma	Sadness	No understanding of life
High Blood Pressure	Mania	Meanness
Headaches	Forgetfulness	Argumentativeness
Neck Pain	Indecisiveness	Quarreling
Back Pain		Anger
Constipation		Fears
Indigestion		Greed
Difficulty Breathing		Jealousy
		Hatred

The Test: Are you a happy person?

I devised the following test based on my knowledge and experience. It gives good insight about oneself. If you do not happen to agree with me on the test, you do have the option not to take it.

I am usually calm in difficult and challenging situations. Y/N

I am fairly content within myself. Y/N

I usually make good decisions and choices. Y/N

I usually do not have to repent for the decisions and choices that I make. If I make a wrong decision, I accept it and then try to fix it. Y/N

I take responsibility for all of my actions/outcomes. Y/N

I do not blame others for any negative outcomes and their results. Y/N

I am open-minded. Y/N

I respect my opinions and also those of others. Y/N

I avoid arguments and quarrels. Y/N

If you have answered most of the question with yes, then you are a happy person. Congratulations! Otherwise it is the time to inquire deeply for an understanding of life. You may also read the chapter again.

The Scale of Happiness: Where do you fit?

It is a well-known fact that happiness and unhappiness are at opposite ends of the spectrum; hence there is a big gap between the two. The majority of people fall into this gap, and you are probably one of them. Now appreciate the extremes:

Always happy (perfect mental balance)

Mentally balanced (good or okay)

Slap happy

Normal

Sad

Depressed

Unhappy, miserable

Now try to analyze to which category you are closest. Take your time. You can try to analyze others as well in this section. This is only to improve your own understanding. You know that no one has any right to judge anyone else.

The Happiness Poem

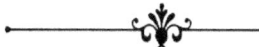

Life is a game that one must learn to play
If one plays it right, it shall be a happy game
Or it can be all misery and pain
Life is a game that one must learn to play
If one plays it right, it will be a happy game

If there is an unhappy ending
One must think with the mighty brain
Where am I wrong and what is wrong?
Don't ever think who else is wrong
It is my life and I am the boss
Do not ever blame the spouse, or the friend
Or it can be all misery and pain

Life is a game that one must learn to play
If one plays it right, it will be a happy game

Happiness is now and here
Don't need to go anywhere
Happiness resides within the heart and soul
Search and find yourself
Don't go crazy like deer musk
Or it can be all misery and pain

Life is a game that one must learn to play
If one plays it right, it will be a happy game

Tomorrow things may not be any different,
But one must learn to play it differently
You better learn this game of life
Or it can be all misery and pain

Life is a game that one must learn to play
If one plays it right, it will be a happy game

Happiness is the desire, need, and want
Our parents, teacher, scriptures, and constitution
Have similar want
Try to understand the need, and not the want
Or it can be all misery and pain

Life is a game that one must learn to play

If one plays it right, it will be a happy game

Happiness is a sure sign of success

One must be clear about this concept

Don't try to find happiness in money, position, or fame

Or it can be all misery and pain

Life is a game that one must learn to play

If one plays it right, it will be a happy game

Happiness is a learnable art

It is no special craft

Nobody is born that smart

Better understand this life's game

Or it can be all misery and pain

Life is a game that one must learn to play

If one plays it right, it will be a happy game

Think what you need today and tomorrow

Not what you could need tomorrow

Look what you have

Not what you could have

There is no end to need, desire or want

Keep the contentment, the only want

Or it can be all misery and pain

Life is a game that one must learn to play

If one plays it right, it will be a happy game

Pain and suffering are part of life

It belongs to every human life

Day and night cannot be separated

Summer and winter are brother and sister

Good and evil often coexist

Health and sickness are not exempt

Understand that you are part of this game

Or it can be all misery and pain

Life is a game that one must learn to play

If one plays it right, it will be a happy game

Pain and suffering are special events

It is an opportunity to get better or best

So that you can pass the final test,

If you fail this test of life

It can be all misery and pain

Life is a game that one must learn to play

If one plays it right, it will be a happy game

This life looks very short,

But we know the soul has no death

And life is an eternal process

Staying on the right path is the final test

So that one can get home (to heaven) safe and sound

This is really not so complex

Try to understand the game of life

Or it can be all misery and pain

Life is a game that one must learn to play

If one plays it right, it will be a happy game

Make friends; make friends, oh my bhai

One never knows when one needs these brothers or bhai

In this or even the next life

Because life is a continuous process

Without a sister, brother, or a friend

It can be all misery and pain

Life is a game that one must learn to play

If one plays it right, it will be a happy game

Anger, hate, jealousy, greed are animal creatures
They kill and eat every brother and sister
These creatures make enemies day and night
One ends up with no brother and sister
When one reaches one's final home (in heaven)?
There will be no one to meet or greet
So better get rid of these creatures
Or life can be all misery and pain

Life is a game that one must learn to play
If one plays it right, it will be a happy game

Happiness is not in money, position, or fame
These are just temporary names
When the body is healthy and intelligent sharp
No one can make one fall apart
When ego is balanced and intellect keen
When the mind is calm and the spirit strong
When the heart is love and the voice is sweet
One wins the game of life
The time is now to understand this game of life
Or it can be all misery and pain

Life is a game that one must learn to play

If one plays it right, it will be a happy game

Make the heart pure and the mind strong

Good words and good acts are the best plan

This is the summary of the final plan

Call me Brother, Singhal, Doctor or Pratap

But take my heartfelt advice

If you want happiness and freedom of life

You better understand the game of life

Or it can be all misery and pain

Life is a game that one must learn to play

If one plays it right, it will be a happy game

Until Next Time — Namaste

I sincerely hope that this book has helped you to raise your happiness level, or at least has prepared you and/or excited you for your long and wonderful journey to a happier life. You must be proud that you have increased the number of happy people in this universe by at least one. Remember, this is an important accomplishment. An important goal of yours and also of this book.

At this moment, I would like to take the opportunity to suggest that, if you believe that this book has benefited you, or has helped you to make some positive changes in your life, please do not put this book back on the shelf. Share, help, and inspire others whom you love and/or respect. It could be anyone, for example, your own spouse, friend, relative, colleague, coworker, doctor, priest, teacher, student, or anyone else. You may even think of giving this book as a gift to them on their birthday, Valentine's Day, Christmas, New Year's Day, and so on. This is another way to help them. Perhaps you may like to donate this book to your local library for the benefit of others. If you are a spiritual person, you know that giving is receiving.

Lastly, I wish to thank you very much for giving me the opportunity to be part of your journey to happiness. I hope to meet you again in one of my next books or other programs.

Pratap C. Singhal

Bibliography

The Art of happiness: His Holiness Dalai Lama, narrated by Howard Cutler.

The happiness equation-- want nothing + to do nothing = have everything. Neil Pasricha.

The Autobiography of a Yogi: Paramahansa Yogananda.

The Bhagwat Geeta, as narrated by Lord Krishna.

Health happiness and you everything you need to know. Pratap C. Singhal MD

Vedic philosophy- the teaching of Hinduism.

The medical histories from my clinic.

Books by the Author

Health, Happiness and You – Everything You Need to Know. [Available in Paperback and E-book]

Live Healthier and Live Happier, with the help of 101+ suggestions, formulas, poems, mantras and lessons learned from short stories. Only paperback.

One Solution to Many Diseases, presented in 24 1/2inspirational stories. [Paperback and e-book.]

Upcoming Books.

How to die. And/or not to die?

Make me younger by the day.

How to reverse the aging and the disease process.

Cancer-How to the prevent and protect from it.

Meditation

Hypertension

www.ingramcontent.com/pod-product-compliance
Lightning Source LLC
Chambersburg PA
CBHW071905290426
44110CB00013B/1282